Wired for
DISRUPTION

Advance Praise

Times of disruption are also opportunities for leaders to evolve and grow. In *Wired for Disruption*, Henna Inam points us to five types of agility that will help each of us not just survive, but thrive in times of relentless change and ambiguity. She reminds us that the key to our thriving is already within our neurobiology and gives us the accelerators to agility.

- Marshall Goldsmith, *New York Times* #1 bestselling author of *Triggers, Mojo*, and *What Got You Here Won't Get You There*.

Adaptation is the key to life. Surviving leaves us feeling empty and with hollow organizations. But adaptation and innovation are impossible without being open to new ideas and exploring possibilities. Henna Inam's *Wired for Disruption* is a thoughtful, exciting, and provocative discussion of recent research and how we can use it in our lives and work. Your future depends on it!

- Richard Boyatzis, Distinguished University Professor, Case Western Reserve University, Co-author of the international best seller, *Primal Leadership* and the new *Helping People Change*.

Henna Inam's *Wired for Disruption* reminds us that disruptions are stressful and disorienting because they challenge our existing mental models. Inam helps leaders visualize a different mindset needed in disruptive times. Her timely and pragmatic book guides leaders to shift their mindsets based on the complexity of the situation at hand. Keep this book at your side — it will be an invaluable companion as you navigate uncertain times.

- Charlene Li, New York Times bestselling author of *The Disruption Mindset* and Founder and Senior Analyst at Altimeter, a Prophet company.

In my view, growing leaders to help them achieve their potential and thrive in change is one of the highest purposes of any organization. Henna Inam's *Wired for Disruption* shares 15 powerful and practical accelerators to help leaders at all levels take accountability for their own growth and also create trusted environments where others can stretch toward their potential.

- Hussain Dawood, Chairman Engro Corp, Dawood Hercules Corp, and Dawood Foundation

In my work with CEOs, what I have found is that the most innovative CEOs always find the opportunity in disruptions. They do that by deeply understanding their stakeholders and influencing their stakeholder ecosystems. In *Wired for Disruption*, Henna Inam points us to neuroscience-based accelerators that enable leaders to create breakthrough growth for their companies and positively impact their ecosystem.

- Mark Thompson, New York Times bestselling author and MG100 #1 CEO Coach

People become open to exploring new possibilities in uncertain times when they have a sense of hope. As Henna Inam puts forth in *Wired for Disruption*, the way leaders can accelerate "neuro-emotional agility" is by creating environments where people can embrace and channel their emotions. The role of the leader in disruptive times is to demonstrate care and engender trust so people become open to imagining new pathways and solutions."

- Laura Tomlin, EVP National Media, E.W. Scripps Company

Looking for the tools and personal insight to ratchet up your leadership impact in this time of disruption? *Wired for Disruption* provides insight to our brain function to teach the keys to outstanding leadership during times of chaos and rapid change. If you are leading a team, large or small, virtual or physical, you will take away some important lessons on listening, experimentation, trust, learning, and coaching to help you develop the ability to lead through disruption.

- Martha Brooks, Corporate Director & Board Co-Chair, CARE USA.

Wired for
DISRUPTION
The Five Shifts in Agility to Lead in the Future of Work

Henna Inam

Copyright

Wired for Disruption: The Five Shifts in Agility to Lead in the Future of Work

Copyright © Transformational Leadership, Inc.

All rights reserved. No part of this book may be reproduced or reprinted in any form or by any means, electronic or mechanical, including photocopying, recording, or by any information storage and retrieval system, without permission in writing from the publisher.

For information regarding permission to reprint material from this book, please mail or email your request to:

Henna Inam
http://www.transformleaders.tv/
Author: Henna Inam
Publisher: Kindle Direct Publishing. Manufactured in the United States of America

Dedication

This book is dedicated to you the reader
Disruption is hard
Yet full of opportunity

To pause
To notice what's here
To deepen connections
To find creativity in chaos
To learn, unlearn and relearn
To widen your lens with curiosity
To find and return to your inner wise self
To tend to all hurts so your heart becomes tender
To step out of your ego and into our collective power
To co-create a better future for all
To re-imagine with fresh eyes
To emerge transformed - a force for good
Now more than ever, our world needs YOU

Table of Contents

Chapter 1 - Our Future Is in Our Hands — 17

Chapter 2 - Neuro-Emotional Agility — 32

Chapter 3 - Learning Agility — 55

Chapter 4 - Trust Agility — 77

Chapter 5 - Stakeholder Agility — 96

Chapter 6 - Growth Agility — 110

Epilogue - My Hope for Our World — 123

Preface

It is January 2020. I have an experience that viscerally shakes me. I am at the World Economic Forum (WEF) in Davos. I happen to walk into a virtual reality experiment. I get handed a seed and told I will experience what it is like to be a tree. Cool! I say to myself. I enjoy hiking and feel a special connection to trees.

The team helps me put on a virtual reality headset and a backpack. I am now under the earth in the soil. I imagine this is what I will see when I'm dead. Cool! I again say to myself. And then realize I probably will not be seeing anything when I'm dead. Soon enough, I burst out of the earth and can see the sunlight through the tall trees around me. There is a giant ant to my left next to a muddy stream of water. I feel myself growing. Then, a tug at my right arm.

As I turn to look at it, I see a beautiful red, green and blue feathered parrot with a long tail has landed there. With a loud squawk the parrot flies off. I hear bird songs around me. Night falls to an awe-inspiring canopy of a million stars so close, I can almost touch them. I breathe deeply to capture this vision in my memory. Everything is alive. Breathing. I feel connected to it all. Everything is as it should be.

As dawn comes, I hear noises in the distance. As the noise becomes louder, I see tractors. Then smoke in the distance. As the sounds of man and machine approach I see trees being burned down. Now the fire is close. I feel heat around my legs. As creatures of the jungle scurry, I hear the panicked squawks of the parrots. The forest is being cut down. The movie stops. I am shaken. Tears in my eyes.

It is May 2020 as I write this. The coronavirus pandemic is sweeping us. It feels like the forest fire. As I write this, there is ambiguity about when a vaccine will become available. There is no ambiguity about how hard and disorienting this is for many of us: stress, anxiety, fear, jobs lost, many deaths. The COVID-19 pandemic feels like it is burning down many existing structures and ways of working. I want to imagine it is clearing space for us to create something new.

I share this story with you because I feel a sense of urgency from which this book is born. Collectively, in the next several months until a vaccine is found, we will be in the heat of disruption. It will have far ranging impacts on how we work, the work we do, and I hope who we become.

Human beings in this decade will face climate disasters, new technology that fundamentally reshapes the work we do, relentless restructuring of the organizations we work within, and for whom we work. These changes have great promise to help us solve meaningful problems such as climate change, disease, poverty and literacy. They also have the potential of peril with hundreds of millions of jobs disrupted, unprecedented levels of stress in the system, increasing wealth inequality, and technology advancing faster than the ethical frameworks to manage it.

In the tenuous gap between promise and peril lies one simple choice, one human at a time. Will you choose to evolve to be a force for good in this disruption? Each of us individually gets to choose where we focus our attention during times of disruption. Our collective future resides in each of our hands. Our world needs each of us to be inspired agents of change to co-create workplaces and a world that works better for all.

If you have any doubt about the power of one individual's choice you will find many stories of heroes and collaborators during this pandemic. Li Wenliang, an ophthalmologist in Wuhan Central Hospital in China was one of the first to raise the alarm about the new virus.[1] He was detained by the authorities and forced to recant his warning. Upon release he went back to treating patients. On February 7, 2020, he succumbed to the disease himself.

We already have within us the wiring to be an agile force for good in times of disruption. My hope is that our collective work and our community will help each of us activate that wiring. This book was supposed to be published at the end of 2020. I've decided to take an agile approach to it and publish it in June 2020. In software, the "agile" approach is used to get early versions out so users can try out the software (bugs and all), give feedback, and improve it for the next release. So here goes. I'm disrupting myself.

I'm also hoping to find collaborators who have a shared mission in reimagining a new future where each person sees themselves a leader, connected to purpose, lending their hands to create a planet that works better for the collective rather than just a few. As you read this book, connect with a change that you want to be part of. Use the accelerators in the book to move toward it. Devote yourself to something bigger than yourself that inspires you. It will change you. As I write this book, I'm reminded of a quote by Tim O'Reilly:

"Pursue something so important that even if you fail, the world is better off with you having tried."

Gratitude

I stand on the shoulders of giants who are devoting their lives to great research and practice in leadership, neuroscience, complexity, mindfulness, and the future of work. They include: Richard Boyatzis, Rick Hanson, Barbara Fredrickson, Otto Scharmer, Kristin Neff, Jennifer Garvey Berger, David Snowden, Susan David and Raj Sisodia.

I have been inspired by my time at the World Economic Forum (WEF) in Davos. This was facilitated by Hussain Dawood, Chairman of the Board of Engro Corporation of which I am an independent director. I was inspired by the many change-makers, dreamers and disruptors at the WEF Future of Work platform coming together to collaborate and imagine a future of work that works better for all.

Many of the people who have helped me include members of the Marshall Goldsmith 100 Group including Mark Thompson, Whitney Johnson, Charlene Li, David Nour, Laine Cohen, Michael Bungay Stanier, Chester Elton, Sarah McArthur, Scott Osman. Our podcast guests have been tremendous sources of learning and inspiration. You can listen to them here (https://transformleaders.tv/podcast/).

So many have helped to input on the ideas in the book including Nahia Orduna, Catherine Brown,

Jimmy Parker, Elizabeth Moran, Vernice Jones, Michelle Prince, Terri Deuel, Ceree Eberly, Jody Pollard, Stacie Torres, and Karstin Bodell.

My executive coaching clients who I cannot name for confidentiality reasons have pressure tested many of the tools in this book and enable me to do work every day that is meaningful for me and helps them move forward in the missions that matter to them.

I'm immensely grateful to our team for their agility. John Fayad helped me edit the book. Jan Louie created graphics. Virtual assistant Pearl Macalley kept it all going!

There are too many to name who have offered their support in our global online community, who gave me feedback on the book title and cover design. I'm truly grateful for the opportunity to co-create with you.

1
Our Future Is in Our Hands

In the middle of every difficulty lies opportunity.
—Albert Einstein, German-born theoretical physicist

The COVID-19 pandemic is teaching us in some very stark ways that in times of disruption the impact of leadership is exponential. Leadership matters. When things are changing quickly, leaders have a magnified impact in shaping the future that emerges. In business model disruptions, it makes a difference in innovation, customer experience, employee engagement and results. In this pandemic disruption, it makes a difference in lives lost.

Whether you're leading yourself, a team of people, an organization, or a country, your agility and that of the people in your charge matters more than ever.

Many of my clients are discovering how their disruption-ready agility makes a difference. Some of them are being called on to lead the way on enterprise-wide response teams because they are seen as leaders who can solve problems in rapid changing situations and have a calming and creative impact. Others are rapidly experimenting, finding opportunity in disruption and shifting their business model. Still others are connecting across their ecosystem to learn and influence with stakeholders to shape a more sustainable future for their business and their industry.

As a board member of a publicly traded company, I interact with board members of companies from across the globe. We see how CEOs who are agile, grounded in purpose and have the skills to influence a wide network of stakeholders are taking charge to have disproportionate impact. Their companies will undoubtedly emerge stronger because they have been agile to listen even more closely to the needs of the moment, to take action and to foster relationships with customers, employees, shareholders, and communities. Company reputations with stakeholders are built or destroyed during disruptions. So are individual and team reputations.

I write this book from the perspective of an executive coach and advisor to senior leaders, a former C-level executive who has led in disruptive environments, a board member and a global citizen. All of these perspectives are grounded in one common mission: to help leaders thrive in times of disruption so together we can create workplaces and a world that work better for all.

Disruption Is Here to Stay

While our world has disrupted, our mindsets, habits, cultures and organization structures are still in the industrial age of predictability and efficiency.

The COVID-19 pandemic crisis we are working through is having far-reaching impacts in terms of after-shocks: consumer behavior, acceleration of digital technologies, mass unemployment, bankruptcies, bailouts, closed borders, and geopolitical shifts. While we yearn for a more predictable world, it seems disruption is here to stay.

We will continue to be in a world where the pace of change and the level of unpredictability leave many of us in threat states and our nervous systems in disarray. Yet, our brain and nervous system are brilliantly wired to be agile. In this book, I will share the switches that *are* in our control to help us thrive in times of disruption.

What Will the Future of Work Look Like?

As of this writing, we are experiencing unprecedented levels of unemployment around the world. Organizations scramble to stay afloat in negative GDP environments. At the same time, social distancing has accelerated digital economies. We will see continued expansion of robotics and artificial intelligence in manufacturing and retail. Our own buying behavior moves further online. These were growing trends that are now embedded in behavior.

In my view, many of the unemployed will find themselves in gig work and many organizations will choose to create teams of a combination of gig workers, external contractors and employees. Organizations will want to create greater business model and cost flexibility. Having experienced pandemic preparedness teams that were created on-demand, our future will include work teams in fluid gig-like arrangements.

It's clear that we need to reskill and upskill people in their digital skills. What is perhaps not so clear yet, is that we need to develop the agility of people at the speed of disruption. We need both will and skill to successfully manage through the disruption in billions of jobs in this coming decade. Each leader individually—and we collectively—need a monumental shift in our ability to take accountability for and manage our own neurobiology, meta-learning, teaming, and growing skills.

As we work in fluid teams both inside and outside organizations, career ladders will be replaced by skills marketplaces. We need to learn how to go from novice to native in any new environment quickly.

As people work in gig economies, it is even more important that they find a deeper sense of meaning in their work. That deeper sense of meaning makes a difference in their own well-being as well as that of the stakeholders they serve. Fear-based choices ("just get a job that provides healthcare.") are a recipe for stress, disengagement, and low customer-experience in the system. As we will learn in Chapter 2, finding meaning is an accelerator to agility.

The implications of all of this is we need institutions (public, private, governments) to partner with each other to create upskilling ecosystems. From our discussions at the World Economic Forum Future of Work initiative, Singapore and Denmark are already creating these ecosystems for their citizens. In April 2020, Coursera, a world-wide online learning platform, stepped forward to help governments upskill their unemployed citizens.[2] We also need each individual to take accountability for their own agility.

We are all searching for what the future will look like and planning for scenarios. In my view, when the way forward is not clear, it is time to pause, imagine and co-create the future we want. The future emerges from our participation in creating it.

What Role Do You Want to Play?

Leadership matters in normal times. In times of disruption, leaders can break down or create breakthroughs with others. When our nervous system is threatened, we can react with survival behaviors that put our own needs above the needs of the many. We forget we are connected and interdependent.

As you will read in the coming chapters, our biology already has the neural connections we need to thrive (not just survive) and be agile in times of change. We just need the accelerators (tools and practices) that help us to create new habits of agility.

Our families, communities, and world need each of us to be empowered agents of change. I believe disruptions are tremendous opportunities for each of us to discover the change that matters to us and co-create it with others. In fact, that is the definition of leadership.

Five Challenges of Leading In Disruption

In history, we've had heads of tribes or rulers who largely made the decisions that impacted many lives. Today, it is people who head up hierarchies in organizations and governments. The model of hierarchy and power of the few is very useful when the focus is on efficiency or when the environment is chaotic. We need an authoritative figure to organize the system.

With unemployment climbing to unprecedented levels, the world is moving toward a gig economy with each human a leader of their work. Each of us are being challenged to bring our human skill sets, creativity, and collaboration to add value. Automation and artificial intelligence are doing repetitive and data-intensive tasks better than humans.

The pandemic has accelerated digital automation, jobs, and whole industry disruptions. This will require millions of us to do different work, leveraging both digital skills and uniquely human skills. Our ways of working in fluid gig-like teams require a shift from a "power over" hierarchical mindset to a "power to" mindset. This requires leaders to engage their people in collective missions that matter to create value and wellbeing.

I believe that there are five challenges for leading in a disruptive environment:

1. Change, unpredictability, and ambiguity put our already stressed nervous systems in threat state.

This impairs our cognition and creativity, creates turmoil in emotions and behaviors, and impacts our outcomes. We can learn to intentionally shift our default neurobiology to calm and creative states. For this, we need *Neuro-Emotional Agility*.

2. High change and unpredictability require a different type of learning. We are now often making decisions in novel situations where there is limited expertise or best practice. We need Learning Agility to widen the view of what we observe, ground ourselves in new realities, question our biases, and shift our mindsets. This meta-learning is not just learning a new skill, it is growing a new brain that increases learning capacity and accelerates our ability to adapt. As the future is unpredictable, we co-create the future by learning in the present moment.

3. Leading in disruption requires quickly creating trust in complex teams. The teams of the emerging future are fluid, globally distributed, multi-generational, often virtual, and span organizational boundaries. We need to build trust quickly to accelerate team performance and well-being. This is *Trust Agility*.

4. The COVID-19 crisis is illuminating just how interdependent we are. We are increasingly solving problems that require shared ownership and action. Problems like pandemic response, climate change, innovating to solve meaningful issues in our ecosys-

tem, or opportunities that require a pivot in business models require us to work with a newer and much wider set of stakeholders than in the past. As we engage with stakeholders with varying and often conflicting needs, we need *Stakeholder Agility* to align this complex system and move toward solutions that work for the whole.

5. Human capacity and agility must be transformed at scale if we are to urgently and effectively solve the meaningful issues to which we are called. This requires that each of us be able to grow ourselves and the people in our ecosystem. This is *Growth Agility*.

The Five Shifts in Agility

Given these challenges to leading in disruptive times, these are the five shifts in agility needed to survive and thrive in the future of work.

1. *Neuro-Emotional Agility* is the ability to recognize, accept, and work through our nervous system reactions in the face of challenge while staying anchored in what matters. It is the ability to activate neural states that accelerate our adaptability.

2. *Learning Agility* is the ability to rapidly learn, unlearn, and re-learn as the reality in front of us changes.

3. *Trust Agility* the ability to develop just-in-time trust with diverse fluid teams and energize creative

Chapter 1 Our Future Is in Our Hands

contributions. It is about broadening our circle of concern from just ourselves to diverse others to enable the best contributions.

4. *Stakeholder Agility* is the ability to identify and influence multiple stakeholders with competing needs toward solutions that serve the broader ecosystem.

5. *Growth Agility* is our ability to grow ourselves and others in high change environments through pivotal conversations and experiments. We grow the capacity and agility of the ecosystem that were operating in. It requires curiosity and humility and creating a shared passion for growing human potential.

As we will learn in the coming chapters, the source of our agility already lies within us. In other words, we are wired to thrive in disruption. As we intentionally switch into neuro-emotional states of calm presence, we can be agile in learning, trusting, influencing stakeholders, and growing ourselves and others. It is in our DNA.

The Five Shifts In Agility

Growth — Learning

Neuro-Emotional

Stakeholder — Trust

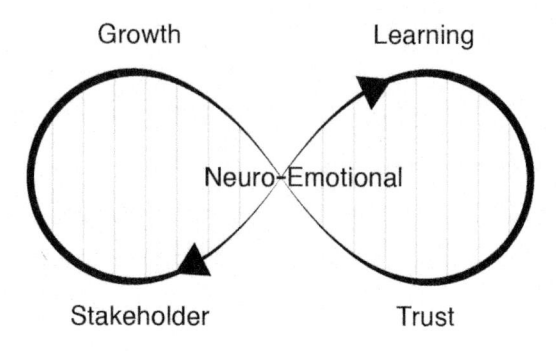

The infinity symbol shows the continuous flow of information and connection between our inner state and our external environment. We shape our environment and are shaped by our environment, and new co-creative possibilities of infinite potential can be created when we begin within.

Growth is Hard

Anyone who regularly sets New Year's resolutions (and then gives up on them six weeks later) knows that changing our own behavior is hard. Knowledge is not a good predictor of behavior. If knowledge predicted behavior, we wouldn't spend billions in smoking cessation and weight loss products (and I would be 20 pounds lighter!).

Our behavior is sticky because it is embedded in our neurobiology, which often operates below our conscious awareness and thinking brain. Our behaviors are a com-

Chapter 1 Our Future Is in Our Hands

plex mix of our neuro-emotional state, our impulses, habits, identity, and what's happening around us.

Mindset Is A Place to Start

So how do we activate our change muscles? It is a combination of motivation and confidence. Motivation comes from a connection with what is intrinsically important to us. It can be a dream or aspiration, or it can be a challenge that is meaningful to us. The human brain is actually wired to learn as novel stimuli cause the brain to release dopamine (a neurotransmitter that is associated with pleasure) which accelerates learning.[3] Confidence often comes from a sense of agency, our actions having some control over our environment. It also comes from being supported by trusted others who point us to our strengths and help us grow.

In the book, I'll share more data about how our biology already has adaptation built into it. As we activate our agility muscles, it's not just good for survival, it will help us thrive! As we activate our agility, we don't simply add new skills to our knowledge bank, we grow the size of the bank. This type of learning is called meta-learning.[4]

The reason disruptions are stress-inducing and disorienting is that they challenge our existing mental models. Our mental model (or mindset) is the unique set of ways we see and make sense of the world. Our mental model is made up of habitual thinking patterns most of which we are not consciously aware of. They

serve a purpose in that they create our identity, a stable picture of assumptions we make about:
- Who we are (our role in our world, the degree of control and agency we have);
- What matters (our inner motivators and drivers); and
- What the world is like (is the world friendly or do I have to be on guard?)

This stable picture is like a polaroid photo. A series of quickly acquired, reinforced over time snapshots of the world as we see it (mostly acquired when we were young). This photo is sticky because stability helps us feel safe. The challenge is that reality is more like a movie. The picture on the screen is always changing.

When disruptions happen, that mental model is challenged because our brain has to work extra hard to reconcile the new reality with the polaroid picture in our brain. It creates cognitive overload and can temporarily cause our brain to shut out the new reality (also called denial). It makes it harder to adapt, harder to solve problems. We get tired more easily. That is, until we grow our agility muscles. The 15 accelerators in this book will help you practice and strengthen your agility muscles.

To Learn, Find Your Inner Explorer

Imagine that you are your favorite scientist or explorer and we're going on a discovery journey together. That serves as a mirror of what we'll actually be doing because throughout our learning together we will be creating new neural pathways in the brain.

We will be asking you to take a deeper dive to examine your mental model, so you can decide what you want to keep; throw out what you don't want; and find new useful parts to experiment with. You're "Marie Kondo-ing" your mindset, referring to a method for tidying up advocated by Japanese organizational consultant, Marie Kondo.[5] Thank your beliefs for serving you when you needed them and discard what you no longer need.

To engage your motivation and confidence, answer these three questions (please take out a piece of paper and write out your answers):

- Imagine your ideal life three years from now, what would be different?
- What is a meaningful challenge for you right now for which this book can help?
- Who is a trusted friend or team member who you'd like to invite to support you in this learning?

Take The Agility Quiz

Are you curious about which of the five types of agility are strengths for you and where you need further development? We have created a short complimentary quiz to help you identify your focus areas. It can be found on our website (https://transformleaders.tv/wiredfordisruption/) and you will receive a customized report and quick tips to strengthen each area of agility.

Our Design Choices with This Book

We've disrupted the traditional book process in writing this book. My team and I are adopting an "agile" approach similar to that used in software development. That means it's shorter than most other business books (what a relief!). It will likely have some bugs, so I'm hoping you will help me make it better (seriously, send your ideas to Collaborate@ TransformLeaders.tv). To deal with the cognitive overload, here are some practical tools:

- Download The 15 Agility Accelerators (actionable tools and checklists) on our website (https://transformleaders.tv/wiredfordisruption/).
- Listen to the Transformational Leadership Podcast (https://transformleaders.tv/podcast/) for deeper dive learning. In these podcast episodes you will hear from experts and practitioners as well as get five-minute coaching exercises to grow yourself and your team.
- Reflection questions and experiments in each chapter. One of the best ways to learn is through learning from experience. As you do these experiments and reflect, you will create new neural agility networks in your brain.

If you're a leader of others, bring these tools to your team so together you can create a more agile culture. We have team learning sprints called the Agility Accelerator Lab (https://transformleaders.tv/wiredfordis-

Chapter 1 Our Future Is in Our Hands

ruption/) so teams can get familiar with the tools and use them. If you're the leader of an organization, I welcome connecting with you to leverage these tools to help your organization become disruption-ready. Welcome to this learning experience together. We hope you'll have fun and share the experience with others!

2
Neuro-Emotional Agility

Between stimulus and response, there is a space. In that space is our power to choose our response.
—Victor Frankl, Austrian Neurologist and Holocaust Survivor

This is how the e-mail from Carlos (we'll call him Carlos to protect the innocent) started:

"Dear Henna,

> *"I wonder if you can help me with the head of one of my sales teams. His name is John. John doesn't think he can sell virtually to our customers during this pandemic. He feels he needs face to face interaction with them. Some of our customers are still trying to figure out how to adapt their business and frankly we're not sure if their business will survive. John is also not confident that our products are a good fit for them now. I'm concerned that his direct reports are floundering without direction. Can you help?"*

The note went on to share an in-depth e-mail that John had sent to Carlos about all the reasons why he needed to wait until things "got better". John (quite dejected) also suggested to Carlos that perhaps he could just retire. I'm sure this was a hard e-mail for John to send. It was a hard e-mail for Carlos to receive because John has been a great leader of his team in the past. He didn't want to lose John. He wanted to help John find his way.

We may know some Johns on our team who are frozen in their response. We may be a Carlos who wants to do well by his people but doesn't know how to help them be more agile. Each of us as leaders of teams and organizations urgently needs team members to quickly respond to and lead the change that is required in disruptions.

Many of my clients who lead teams and organizations notice the difference in performance between those who are agile and those who are not. Their challenge is "I know how to be agile. I just don't know how to make John more agile". Most of us haven't really been trained on how to move ourselves and others from this state of fragility we sometimes feel to a state of agility. In this chapter we will learn how to do this.

Organizations in the last few years collectively spent over $100 billion dollars in digital transformation. Data shows that at least 50 percent of transformations fail. The money might as well have been burned. Worse, it left many people burned out. Digital transformations fail not because of the technology but because of human capacity to be agile to change.[6]

What if you could find a way to save the money, help people be agile and actually promote well-being? The answer lies in Neuro-Emotional Agility. Peeking inside the brain (literally) using Functional Magnetic Resonance Imaging (fMRI) to discover the areas being 'lit up' by movement of blood flow, we can discover what makes people agile. We have the switch within us.

What is Neuro-Emotional Agility

Neuro-Emotional Agility is the ability to recognize, accept, and work through our nervous system reactions in the face of challenge while staying anchored in what matters. It's also about recognizing when others are in threat states and creating safety so they can feel supported while they are stretched.

In fact, the greater the stretch we feel, the greater the support we need in order to be agile and to learn and grow from an experience. We start here because our neurobiology impacts our behaviors and our outcomes. In the previous chapter we discussed how our habitual mindsets are created over years of thinking the same thoughts. These trigger emotions that drive behavior.

Think

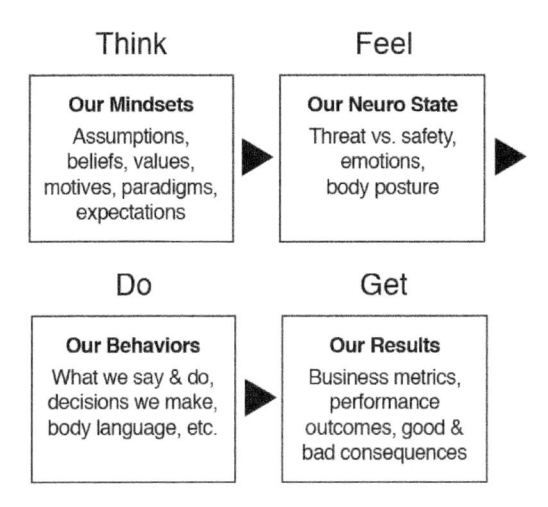

Our Mindsets
Assumptions, beliefs, values, motives, paradigms, expectations

Feel

Our Neuro State
Threat vs. safety, emotions, body posture

Do

Our Behaviors
What we say & do, decisions we make, body language, etc.

Get

Our Results
Business metrics, performance outcomes, good & bad consequences

It's mission critical in disruptions because our brain and nervous system get in high-threat mode. For some of us this threat mode propels us to take action to respond to the threat. It concentrates the mind wonderfully. For many others it can disorient or freeze us. Or we get into action that is without focus. Instead, we need to intentionally shift ourselves to a creative and generative state. As you will see in this chapter, this generative state is actually good for our well-being.

Our nervous system evolved to ensure survival so it has a negative bias. Survival depended on our ability to make predictions, especially related to avoiding threats. This threat system is actually very useful. The challenge is that it becomes quick-to-trigger over time. Our brain doesn't like environments where it doesn't have the ability to predict or control.

The amygdala, found in the reptilian or oldest part of our brain, interprets change as a threat to the body and its homeostasis, and releases hormones to prepare for fight, flight, or freeze responses. As these kick in, our reasoning brain fades into the background. That is one of the reasons why when presented with a new idea or initiative, many people will initially resist. Why disturb the comfortable familiarity of status quo?

When our nervous system feels threatened, it is harder to see the full picture of reality and to adapt to changes. In fact, under threat, our peripheral vision actually diminishes as we hyper-focus on the threat in front of us. Threat states reduce cognition, curiosity and creativity. These states can cause us to unconsciously slip into controlling behaviors such as hoarding information, silo thinking, and micromanaging others. Worse yet, our neuro-emotional state is not just a key driver of our own decision-making,[7] it also impacts those around us because our emotions are contagious.[8]

As we (unconsciously) think the same thoughts over the course of years in many instances, these get imprinted in the brain with emotions and even body postures. They become part of our habitual mindset and identity. These habitual mindsets impact behaviors which create predictable patterns in our relationships and our outcomes.

Our neuro-emotional state also impacts our

in-the-moment responses. When we feel under threat, our sympathetic nervous system gets activated and cortisol and adrenaline flood the body. This increases heart rate, oxygen to the lungs, and blood flow to the muscles. Our posture may change to become bigger (when in fight mode) or smaller (in flight or freeze mode). We may experience a dry mouth, our palms may become sweaty, our tone of voice may change. Our body may become tense. We breathe differently.

The threat response can be quite personal as well. Some people might freeze and become more lethargic. The key is to notice your own personal threat response so you can be mindful of when you're in threat mode. In the story at the beginning of this chapter, our friend John is likely in a classic "freeze" mode. My podcasts at the end of this chapter with neuroscience researcher Richard Boyatzis and somatic coach Amanda Blake go into depth about these neural states and the practices you can experiment with to reduce threat state in your body.

When we calm ourselves to get to a safe state, we are able to notice more and are open to others' ideas and experiences. We are able to be more curious, concerned, caring, and playful. Our capacity to reflect increases and our peripheral vision expands. Training our nervous system to recover quickly allows us to be more anchored even in challenging times.

Neuro-Emotional Agility Challenges

While each of us has a different capacity for being adaptive in change, we do go through a general process when confronted with any kind of change. The Kubler Ross change curve describes the process of "grieving" that we go through when confronted with change.[9]

The Kubler Ross change curve is based on research about grieving. We often experience denial at the start as our brain tries to hold on to the familiar world. In a change process, this curve helps us grieving the loss of the old. As we integrate the new, we go through various emotional states until we can find acceptance and meaning. Of course, while this curve is directionally correct for any individual and circumstance, it cannot be predictably timed or controlled.

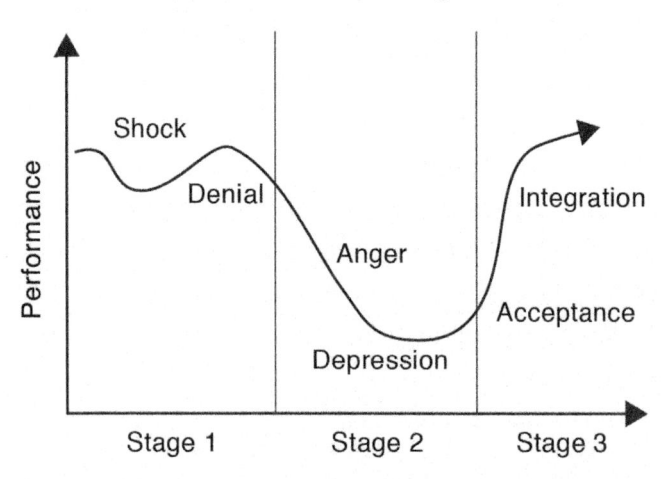

The Kübler-Ross Change Curve

Chapter 2 Neuro-Emotional Agility

The challenge for most of us (particularly in a workplace context) is that we are not great at managing our emotions or those of others. Workplaces typically don't teach us how to handle emotions because emotional behaviors are considered taboo at work. Many of us cope with difficult emotions by suppressing them or denying them. The cost of ignoring our emotions is that they build up and eventually leak out at inopportune times in stressful situations. It also takes vital energy to suppress an emotion or to numb ourselves. This saps creativity and well-being.

A challenge for teams is that each team member may be at a different place in their adaptation to any given change. Often, we don't know where others are because our current workplace mindset and norm is to not discuss emotions at work. We want others to hurry up and be where we are, or slow down and be where we are. Instead we need to practice meeting people where they are and with empathy and compassion.

This "emotional hijack" is a normal part of being human. Different human beings go through the change curve at different paces. The change curve is directionally correct rather than predictive in a time period or even in a specific person. Getting to acceptance cannot be forced from the outside. As we will see in the accelerators, finding meaning and positive purpose in the change is what helps us accelerate our change curve.

Neuro-Emotional Agility Accelerators

To shift toward adaptive behaviors here are three accelerators that help clients through this process.

Accelerator 1: Activate Empathy

Just like our nervous system activates for survival under threat, it also has a way to calm down to think clearly, be creative and adapt. That's the empathic neural network and that is connected with the Parasympathetic Nervous System (PNS) of the body.

The Vagus Nerve (part of the PNS), is the longest nerve in the nervous system of our bodies and affects all major organs and their functioning.[10] This includes heart rate, blood pressure, breathing, and the release of anti-stress hormones. The Vagus is also called the nerve of emotion and impacts whether we feel safe and protected.

Practices that immediately give the body a signal that we are no longer under threat include long deep breaths from the belly. Specifically, when we elongate our exhale, it relaxes us, activating the PNS, improving the health of the Vagus Nerve (called vagal tone).[11]

Try it now! (Yes, I mean now, see how you feel after three long exhales).

Additionally, studies show that yoga increases parasympathetic nervous system activity thereby improving vagal tone and overall health.

Chapter 2 Neuro-Emotional Agility

Another way to calm down our nervous system is to slow down and turn our attention inward with compassion for ourselves. With now over 2,600 studies on self-compassion, research shows that self-compassion is a key driver of resilience. Research from Dr. Kristin Neff, author of the book *Self-Compassion* points to the data that brains can be trained for compassion.[12] When we train our brain for self-compassion, it is easier to tune into difficult emotions we may be feeling and respond with care.

Research shows that self-compassion practice helps us stretch to take more risks, as well as extends the compassion we feel for others. It doesn't make us weaker; it makes us stronger and more agile. You can listen to Dr. Neff talking about her research as well as experience her guided self-compassion practice on our podcast at the end of this chapter.

To practice mindful self-compassion, tune into your body. It takes just five minutes or less. Find a quiet space. Take a few deep breaths feeling your lower belly rise and fall. Lengthen your exhale. Long exhales activate our parasympathetic nervous system which helps us feel calm and relaxed. We notice the body sensations and emotions as they come into our awareness. We label them and practice being with them with acceptance and compassion. Here's what an inner landscape check might sound like if we are speaking our experience out loud:

> *"I'm noticing that my shoulders are tense, I'm noticing that my breath is shallow, I'm noticing a feeling of anxiety in my stomach… and so on. This is a difficult moment. Difficult moments are part of being human, may I be kind to myself".*

To experience this, take the five-minute "Emotional Resilience" podcast at the end of this chapter. Our emotional landscape is rich and has beautiful clues to connect deeper with what is meaningful for us. As we repeat this practice, we develop greater sensitivity to our body's signals.

This helps us develop greater sensitivity to others' emotions as well so we can be more emotionally intelligent in our actions. Of course, in order to do this, we actually need to slow down. Slowing down in itself and focusing on one thing at a time has a positive impact on our well-being.

Mindfulness (of which I am a fan and over a decade long practitioner) actually helps strengthen our nervous system to prevent these threat hijacks. What creates emotional turmoil during disruptions are our racing thoughts and fears about the future. With mindfulness, we develop a friendly awareness of the present. As we drop into the present and observe our racing thoughts, we are not as impacted by them because we are an "observer" of thoughts. It's a bit like watching a horror movie from 20 rows back rather than feeling like we're in it! With our awareness in the present moment, we realize that right now we're safe and okay.

Just an eight-week practice lowers the size of the amygdala (our fast threat alert brain) and increases the pre-frontal cortex (our rational thinking and problem-solving brain).[13] This means that practitioners of mindfulness are actually able to strengthen and insulate their nervous system so it becomes more able to quickly recover and be resilient in the face of neuro-emotional threats.

Practices like mindfulness or breathing deeply are a great way to build a resilient nervous system over time. They also can offer an immediate fix. This becomes even more critical when we are outside our comfort zones. We learn to breathe and stay calm in difficult moments and conversations.

As we do this, we grow new neural networks and possibilities for ourselves and our environment. We are able to move in a more empowered way toward what matters. Even as our body feels threatened outside our comfort zone, we can take a stand for what matters because we activate our empathic neural network. And over time, we expand the range of situations where we remain calm under threat.

Accelerator 2: Get Curious About Your Story
Once the body has regained a sense of safety, the next step is to get curious. A tool I have used with executive coaching clients is the Mind Story Map™.

It helps leaders take a mental step back to notice their own mindset. When we step back to notice what is happening in our mind and body, it actually helps us see the patterns that keep us stuck. It allows us to create new possibilities.

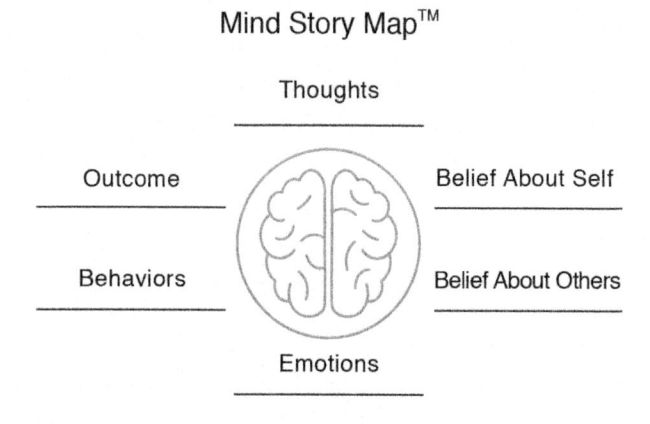

Mind Story Map™

```
                    Thoughts
                    _____

   Outcome                      Belief About Self
   _____                     _____

   Behaviors                    Belief About Others
   _____                    _____

                    Emotions
                    _____
```

We start anywhere on the map that is most present for a leader. We notice the emotion, notice a set of thoughts and beliefs associated with the emotion, and we see the actions and outcomes as a result. This tool helps leaders widen the lens of what they are seeing. Instead of being at the effect of their thoughts, in essence, being a prisoner of their thoughts, they can now get curious, rise above the emotion, and recognize their own habitual patterns.

Labeling feelings allows a different part of the brain to come to the forefront. We step back, we notice patterns, and we can make a different choice because we see more than we saw before.

Chapter 2 Neuro-Emotional Agility

Recently, an executive coaching client, frustrated by the lack of information-sharing during a large restructuring in his organization, was able to use this Mind Story Map ™ to shift his neuro-emotional state. He saw how his thought pattern of "I don't have enough information to share with my team. The CEO is making a mess of this" was keeping him stuck. When he saw this pattern, he was able to see how his "victim mindset", as he later called it, was not who he really was or aspired to be.

Indeed, at the root of his frustration was a sense of caring for the people he led. He realized he had control about how he communicated with his own team. He had control over his own mindset. As he saw the pattern, he was able to see possibilities outside the pattern.

Once we see a pattern, we start to notice it more in our daily behavior. Then we have a choice. We can shift toward our more aspirational selves.

Accelerator 3: Find Purpose

Research conducted over the past 30 years by Richard Boyatzis, Distinguished Professor at Case Western Reserve University and co-author of *Helping People Change*, suggests that the best way to help others change is to activate the Empathic Neural Network in the brain.[14] His research is based on 39 longitudinal studies of behavior change improving emotional, social and cognitive intelligence actions, three fMRI studies and two hormonal studies. It shows that activating the Empathic Neural Network in our brains is what helps human beings change. We are already wired to be agile. Becoming mindful of our threat states and activating the neural networks that bring calm is the key to unlocking that agility.

Our brain operates in two neural networks. The Analytic Neural Network is task-focused and best used for focused tasks, problem solving and setting goals. The Empathic Neural Network allows us to have greater concern for others, act with greater integrity, and be more agile to change. When we are in this state, we are more open to others' new ideas and thinking and we are more adaptive to change.

The Analytic and Empathic networks often seesaw. When one is present, the other is not. Many of us spend most of our time at work in goal-setting, task-focused, and analytical activities. These are also the brain states that are involved in many of our team conversations. While this neural network is necessary for solving problems, activating the Empathic Neural Network in ourselves and others is what helps us be more open to change.

Boyatzis's research shows that some of the best ways to activate the Empathic Neural Network is to direct our attention to positive emotion inducing activities. For example, when working with leaders he asks:

- "If your life and work were ideal, what would it be like in 10-15 years?"

- "Who helped you the most in your life become who you are or get to where you are?"

These questions activate the imagining part of our brain and gratitude, both of which open us up to curiosity and learning.

Another critical element in his research (which was conducted in the context of helping people in coaching environments change) includes building a caring and trusting relationship. It speaks to the importance of having trusted others who provide vital support and safety as we stretch. We of course know this from teachers and other people who have supported us.

Take a moment now to reflect on your answers to the questions above. Notice if this reflection creates a shift in your own neuro-emotional state.

Finding Purpose in Disruption

In his classic book *Man's Search for Meaning*, Holocaust survivor Victor Frankl famously said, "Those who have a 'why' to live, can bear with almost any 'how'". There is neuroscience that supports this. Finding meaning actually releases the hormone oxytocin in our brains.[15] This hormone is associated with our Empathic Neural Network creating agility, trust and cooperation.

Finding our purpose within the disruption is an accelerator to our agility because it helps us accept what's presented to us, find meaning in it, and accelerate integration (Stage 3 of the Kubler-Ross Change Curve presented earlier). When we find a way to contribute within what's happening, we become part of the change. In times of ambiguity, leaders can create clarity by pointing to shared purpose and also help each individual connect with their own sense of meaning and purpose.

The Purpose Accelerator™ is a simple tool with which accomplish this. We look for the sweet spot among three aspects of our experience as illustrated below. We look back to the most meaningful times in our lives to discover what fulfills and energizes us. Who were we being then? What impact were we having on others? We look to the strengths and resources that we already have. We look to the stakeholders that matter in this current context to understand their needs.

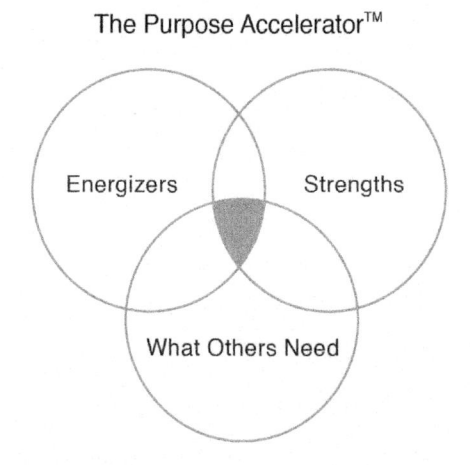

The Purpose Accelerator™

Energizers | Strengths

What Others Need

As we pause to consider these questions, our unique contribution emerges. We can create a purpose statement by addressing how we create value for

Chapter 2 Neuro-Emotional Agility

others that also inspires us. For example, my purpose statement is: *To help grow people toward their highest impact so together we create workplaces and a world that work better for all.*

Take a few minutes to think through this for yourself or connect with your team or accountability partner to do this together.

Your purpose statement is not fixed. Mine continues to evolve. It is like a North Star to help guide me, especially in times of ambiguity, when visibility is low. Focusing on purpose helps us feel empowered and resilient in change. It lowers threat level and gives us a feeling of being in control. It helps us to come back when our neurobiology throws us off course. It is a powerful anchor for how we interact with others as we go through change together. We ask ourselves how we can bring our best and most purposeful selves to our interactions with people around us as we confront challenges together.

For a deeper dive, there is a "Purpose" accelerator podcast that may prove helpful to you at the end of this chapter. It will help you connect with your contribution in change. As we get into the disruptive future of work, purpose can be a powerful compass with which to navigate the skills we want to develop, and a guide to the work projects and jobs that will be meaningful.

Accelerator 4: Listen Well

Each of us already has an empathy system in our brains. This system causes us to be sensitive to and recognize each other's emotions. Moreover, we can often unconsciously mirror each other's behavior. When someone yawns in a room, it triggers yawning in others. This empathetic system explains how and why laughter yoga (an exercise involving prolonged voluntary laughter), or mob behavior, or a stressed-out boss impacts us. This is why we start with ourselves first.

Once we are ourselves in a place of calm, our work as leaders is to help others adapt to change. The best way to do that is to start by meeting them where they are. Because emotions are often taboo in the workplace and we're not really trained to be therapists, it can be hard to approach peoples' emotional lives. Many of us don't want to open a can of worms that we feel ill-equipped to handle.

Many of us are getting experience checking in with each other during these pandemic times. One simple question we can ask is "how are you now?" and then just listen. Others' emotions, no matter how uncomfortable they make us feel, or how much we care about them, are not a problem to be fixed. (Trust me, I've tried!). Just practice being with them without trying to uplift them or justify their emotion or negate their emotion.

Seriously, mute yourself! Our deep and compassionate listening has tremendous value to others

Chapter 2 Neuro-Emotional Agility

because it creates a safe space for them. You will know when there is space to speak. In that space, it is simply okay to let them know that you understand what they are going through. Acknowledging fear, anxiety, or other challenging emotions as a normal part of the human experience creates safety for others which in turn helps create trust and agility.

Listening deeply also accelerates our own agility. It's particularly useful when we're empathizing with others. There are four levels of listening that Otto Scharmer (MIT Senior Lecturer) talks about in his transformative edX course "Leading from the Emerging Future".[16] Most of us operate at Level 1 and Level 2 most of the time. We are listening to confirm what we know or learn new data or facts. As we reach higher levels of listening (Levels 3 and 4) we learn more and are able to adapt to the situation we are in. When we're empathizing with others, we are listening at Level 3.

Just for a few moments, we set aside our own needs. With complete fascination about their experience, we step into how others see the world. We're paying attention to their tone, body language, facial expressions, energy, and emotion. We're listening to what is said and what is unsaid. We listen to help others feel safe, seen, heard, understood.

Four Levels of Listening

Level	Intent	Focus On	Sounds Like
Level 1 Hearing	To contribute what I already know	**My Competence** What I already know, how I'm right, how to fix their problem	"I know, I get it..." "I was right..." "You should..."
Level 2 Seeing	To find new data	**Their Content** Words, numbers, facts past experience (external realities)	"I didn't know that!" "Wow, look at that!"
Level 3 Feeling	To relate	**Their Concerns** Tone, body language, facial expressions, rate/volume of speech, energy (internal realities)	"You seem..." "How do you feel about..."
Level 4 Intuiting	To learn, grow, and be steered to new solutions	**Larger Context** Includes the ecosystem including me, interdependencies	"I didn't realize..." "I learned..." "How about we..."

Micro-Behaviors for Neuro-Emotional Agility

1. Checks in several times a day to notice their own feelings
2. Accepts own emotions with compassion
3. Checks in with others and creates a safe space for others to share their emotions.
4. Handles others' emotions with compassion
5. Finds ways to be purposeful within a changing environment.

Questions for Reflection

1. As you consider a disruption in your situation, where are you now in your own change curve? Where are others on your team? What do they need from you?
2. Use the "Purpose" podcast (link below) to discover a contribution you're inspired to make.
3. What new opportunities open up when you consider purpose?

Experiments to Try

1. Check in with yourself several times a day. You can try a five-minute practice to *Calm The Mind* on LinkedIn Learning from my course "Mindfulness Practices at Work"(https://www.linkedin.com/learning/mindfulness-practices/becoming-mindful-at-work).
2. Try the *Emotional Resilience* podcast (https://transformleaders.tv/emotional-resilience/) to process emotions. What did you learn?
3. Pick one action to bring your unique contribution to the disruption you're in. What did you learn?
4. Practice listening at Level 3 in one conversation. What did you discover?
5. Create a vision board with pictures to envision your ideal future. Connect with that and your purpose every day.

Additional Resources

1. Podcast with Dr. Richard Boyatzis (https://transformleaders.tv/richard-boyatzis/) on helping people change.

2. Podcast interview with Amanda Blake (https://transformleaders.tv/amanda-blake/) on somatic practices to recover from threat states.

3. Podcast interview with Kristin Neff (https://transformleaders.tv/kristin-neff/) on self-compassion.

4. Purpose (https://transformleaders.tv/purpose-podcast/) podcast (Episode 17) to help you discover your contribution in change.

3
Learning Agility

The illiterate of the 21st century will not be those who cannot read or write, but those who cannot learn, unlearn, and relearn.
—Alvin Toffler, American Writer & Futurist

Learning Agility in times of disruption is the ability to learn quickly from our experience and create new mindsets and behaviors that move us toward what matters. In disruption, we need to learn at the pace of change; be open to challenging and shifting our own mindset and biases; and be open to new experiences and experiments that push us outside our comfort zone.

In order to do this, we need to learn differently. We grow our capacity to learn through meta learning.

This is not about learning concepts, what are known and proven, or learning skills such as how to be a better communicator or trained in big-data analysis or coding. These skills are of course important. In disruptive environments, there is more complexity and often no "best practice". Our school systems and early experiences often create mindsets in us to search for the "right answer". We get A's by acquiring knowledge (what is known). Yet, in disruptive times such as the one we are now experiencing because of the pandemic, we are now operating in environments where much is unknown. It's not useful to operate from our past assumptions because the now and the future are not like the past.

Our default mindset of learning is in learning a concept. In school, we are rewarded for finding the one "right answer" to a problem. We're rewarded with getting A's, having a good GPA, and getting the "right answers" in standardized testing which set us up for supposedly brilliant careers.

We are also rewarded for learning skills (e.g. how to speak better in public, how to code) and we're rewarded for growing this skill. In the digital future of work, we need the ability to rapidly learn new skills. In my view, the future of work will require us to expand our Learning Agility by:

- Widening the lens to see different contexts for making decisions.
- Rapidly shifting our own mindsets to the context we are in.
- Learning swiftly by doing experiments, asking different questions, reflecting and imagining an emerging future we want to be part of, rather than just knowledge or skills.

Challenges of Learning in Disruption

There are two main challenges of learning in times of disruption.

First, as we know our nervous system gets hijacked

when we feel under threat. It prevents us from seeing the full picture and understand that the context that we're operating in has changed. And the context has indeed changed. There is less predictability than in our previously "known" world. These situations are called "Complex" as in the figure below, and require us to widen our lens and recognize how complex problems require different mindsets to solve them.

Second, in disruptive environments, our brain biases are actually exacerbated due to our threat state, preventing us from accurately seeing the new reality. We therefore need to rapidly shift to seeing the new and emerging reality so we may make the best decisions possible.

Learning Agility Accelerators

In my view, there are three important Learning Agility accelerators.

Accelerator 1: Match Mindset to Complexity

In disruptive environments there can be a mismatch of mindsets. Our habitual mindsets seek a right or wrong answer or some best practice to lean on in order to find safety in times of disruption. A Learning Agility move is to instead take a step back to widen the lens and assess the situation we are dealing with.

A great way to visualize a different type of learning needed during disruption is through the Cynefin Framework (see figure below). *Cynefin*, pronounced ku-*nev*-in, is the Welsh word for habitat and the events in our experience that influence us in ways we can never fully understand.

The framework was created by European IBM director David Snowden in 1999 along with his colleague Mary E. Boon to provide decision-makers a context and perspective from which to not only make better decisions but also avoid the problems that arise when their default management style causes them to make mistakes. [17]

The Cynefin Framework

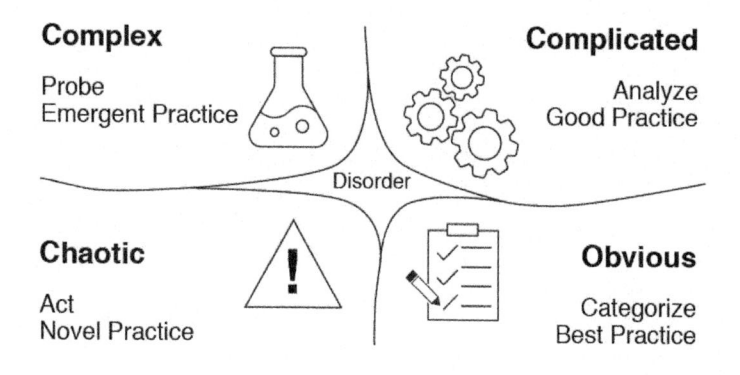

Complex
Probe
Emergent Practice

Complicated
Analyze
Good Practice

Disorder

Chaotic
Act
Novel Practice

Obvious
Categorize
Best Practice

The framework categorizes the issues facing leaders into four primary contexts as defined by the nature of the relationship between cause and effect. Four of these contexts—Obvious, Complicated, Complex, and Chaotic—guide leaders to evaluate situations and to act in ways appropriate to each context.

In an "Obvious" context, there are tight constraints,

options are clear, and the cause-effect relationships are apparent to everyone. Even in disruptive environments, the right answer is self-evident. The decision-making approach is to determine the problem, categorize it to come to the right solution, and respond. Automatic call centers, for instance, route customer calls to the appropriate resources based on customer responses. In the case of COVID-19, there is best practice that washing your hands and wearing masks lowers your risk of spreading the infection.

"Complicated" problems might have several right solutions. There's a clear relationship between cause and effect, but it may not be visible to everyone. The decision-making approach here is to assess the situation, analyze what is known—often with the help of experts—and decide on the best response using good practice. In the case of COVID-19, a "Complicated" problem being solved is how the U.S. Food & Drug Administration (FDA) can accelerating their process to put anti-viral therapies into clinical trials.

In a "Complex" context there is less predictability. Cause and effect are not necessarily linear and often can only be assessed in retrospect. Complex contexts are actually already part of our everyday experience. They include changing culture in an organization or getting your teenager to clean their room. This is because changing human behavior is often unpredictable and there are many influences in the system.

The decision-making approach here is to step back to fully see the situation, probe it from many different perspectives because cause and effect are not so obvious, probe for causes and patterns, sense for developing solutions, and respond with an Emerging Practice. The founders of Uber, for instance, never imagined the effect their fledging company and the "ride-sharing" category they ultimately created, would have on the taxi industry and the emergence of their food delivery service, Uber Eats.

In a "Chaotic" landscape, the relationship between cause and effect are impossible to determine because they shift and no identifiable patterns exist. Searching for the "right" answer in this chaotic environment is ineffective. A leader's immediate responsibility is to act to establish order, then respond by working to transform the situation from chaos to complexity, where the identification of emerging patterns and practices can organically reveal themselves. The effect COVID-19 is having on world health and the global economy in a very short period of time, and the novel practices in public-private partnerships to solve for Personal Protection Equipment (PPE) shortages falls into this category.

These charts focus on the "Complex" domain where many disruptions challenge us.

Chapter 3 Learning Agility

Complexity of Problem

Predictable ←——————————————————→ Unpredictable

OBVIOUS
Future is like past, "autopilot" reactions are very efficient

- Problem is clear
- Follow best practice

COMPLICATED
Future is like past, expertise helps predict, control, redesign

- Problem is clear
- Look for data & experts to help find the solution.

COMPLEX
Future is uncertain, expertise can hurt

- Challenge may be unclear
- Get curious about what works and what doesn't
- Challenges to be managed rather than concrete problems to be solved.

Our minds prefer simplicity and predictability. In fact, our educational systems have prepared us to learn that there are right and wrong answers and if we're asking too many questions or questioning the teacher's authority we are being disrespectful. Yet, disruptions often throw us in complex and unpredictable situations. The challenges are often unclear and the solutions are outside our control.

We must shift to a different mode. It's very much like how our body uses muscles differently when we are climbing uphill vs. walking on flat ground. This is a brilliant opportunity to activate a different part of our neurobiology, our Empathic Neural Network, to get curious, to connect with others, to try experiments, to fail quickly and to try something else. We ask different questions.

Chapter 3 Learning Agility

Match Mindset To Complexity

Predictable ←——————————————→ Unpredictable

OBVIOUS
Future is like past, "autopilot" reactions are very efficient

- What's the best practice?

COMPLICATED
Future is like past, expertise helps predict, control, redesign

- Who are the right experts?
- What analysis needs to be done?

COMPLEX
Future is uncertain, expertise can hurt

- What's the challenge?
- What assumptions are we making?
- How could we be wrong?
- What are diverse perspectives?
- What's the right experiment?

When we're operating in the Obvious" domain, there is a right and wrong answer and knowledge and efficiency create value. On the other hand, in the "Complex" domain, expertise can be dangerous because it can make us over-confident. Instead, curiosity, learning, diversity of perspectives, and experimentation is valuable. Our default mindsets and desire to "get it perfect" or "be right" or "avoid failure" can get in the way of learning quickly.

Accelerator 2: Check & Declare Bias

It is said that Artificial Intelligence (AI) experts are now teaching computers to come up with better questions than humans can ask of them, across a variety of subjects, for the simple reason that we are not as good as we think at identifying the gaps in our knowledge. Another way of expressing these gaps in awareness is that we don't know what we don't know. There will always be gaps in our knowledge, places where we are absolutely clueless about our ignorance.

A part of us may want to feel like it knows all there is to know (to reduce threat levels), but given our common biases, we often prevent ourselves from closing these knowledge gaps. In fact, many poets and philosophers refer to this not knowing what we don't know as a place of mystery and infinite possibility. This is the place of creativity and potential.

In a disruption we need to rapidly shift to seeing the new and emerging reality. It may be a new competitor just on the horizon. It may be an emerging customer need or a completely new customer we haven't served before. The human brain however fails to see this because of our biases. While reality is changing as in a movie, our brain is processing it as a polaroid camera. The movie and storyline have advanced and we are still at the first frame of the picture. This is due to common human biases encoded in our DNA's primary function which is to survive.

The Source of Bias

In 2005, the National Science Foundation (NSF), an independent agency, published an article summarizing research on human thoughts per day. It was found that the average person has about 12,000 to 60,000 of them. and of those thousands of thoughts, 80 percent are negative, and 95 percent are exactly the same recurring thoughts as the day before. [18]

It takes a great of energy to process all of our 60,000 thoughts on a daily basis. While the brain represents on average just two percent of our total body weight, while at rest, our brain uses up 20 to 25 percent of the body's overall energy, mainly in the form of glucose. [19]

In an effort to conserve calories (this was in the days prior to the McDonald's meal deals) and function efficiently in the world, the mind is designed to filter out much of the information coming at us. A massive amount of information constantly floods the senses, and we must have the ability to focus on what's important and be able to tune out the rest.

Researchers have actually pinpointed a circuit in the brain, a thin layer of inhibitory neurons called the Thalamic Reticular Nucleus (TRN), that suppresses distracting and irrelevant data.[20] Researchers believe that when one part of the human brain is engaged, the other parts have less energy to handle their own basic tasks such as in reasoning and remembering. This is why we may be more forgetful when under stress or even have lapses in memory and "blank out" during shocking or emotionally disturbing events.[21] This is also why learning is challenging and Learning Agility is highly critical during times of disruption.

Our biases are hardwired into our brain, which evolves for the constant survival of the species. Our brain scans for threats and "rules" as a way to make sense of the world. These rules then become shortcuts that form biases. The problem is not that we have biases; the problem is that we're often unaware of them. The work of Learning Agility is then to check our biases and not assume that we're always right. To make matters more challenging, our biases are exacerbated under threat conditions as we enter a defensive state and our peripheral vision declines.

If you have a free day and are fascinated by biases as I am, take a stroll through Wikipedia's list of hundreds of well-documented brain biases.[22] If you have a bias for simplicity, there are five that are artfully articulated in Jennifer Garvey Berger's book *Unlocking Leadership*

Chapter 3 Learning Agility

Mindtraps.[23] Berger is an expert in leading in complex environments. In her book, she states that "Humans are brilliantly designed – for an older, less-connected, and more predictable version of the world." Here are the biases she cites:

Bias for Simplicity: We prefer easy stories and simple explanations. This goes back to our evolutionary brain bias to prioritize survival. We needed to conserve calories and filter out unnecessary information. We want to believe in a world of cause and effect and know that we have the rule book for it. So, we make up simple stories (our ways of seeing the world) and believe that we're seeing the world as it is.

Instead we are seeing the world as we are, through the blinders of our own mindset. Psychologists have long used the famous Rorschach Inkblot Test to see how their patients make meaning of the world.[24] Different people see different images in the same inkblot. Try it sometime at your favorite family gathering!

What this suggests is that we can be in the same meeting and take away different conclusions (something I'm sure has never happened to you!). This means we project our own beliefs onto the future ("It will stay how it was in the past") and onto others' motivations ("He didn't reply to my e-mail, so I must not be so important").

Bias to Be Right: We tend to notice what we believe. This confirms to us that we are right. This is confirmation bias. When we want a certain idea or concept to be true (i.e. it serves our paycheck or view of the world) we end up believing it to be true (e.g. "I'm much smarter than the average person). This bias leads us to stop gathering information. We Google something and pick the first link that confirms our beliefs. We embrace information that confirms our view while ignoring information that refutes it. In times of disruption, it may prevent us from seeing what has changed.

Bias to Belong: In our deep history, it helped to be part of a tribe and be supported by them. Our wiring is therefore to be agreeable. We agree because we want to get along with others who are like us. We also tend to pay more attention to and believe those like us, preventing us from seeing the perspective of others who are different from us. This creates echo chambers in social media, political discourse, team meetings, and board rooms. In Complex situations this prevents us from seeing the full picture of what's really going on.

Bias for Control: We like to be in control of our world;

Chapter 3 Learning Agility

it helps us feel safe. This is especially true in disruptions. We want to pull in the reins or at least believe we are in control. This doesn't work because we don't know the cause and effect in a Complex environment.

Ego Biases: Our ego can freeze us in place and prevent our growth because we create an identity and stick to it. Our identity is a set of mindsets that is created based on personality preferences and childhood experiences. It defines our comfort zone. In disruptions we may want to cling even more to our sense of identity because it makes us feel safe and less lost. In my podcast with Jennifer Garvey Berger (available at the end of this chapter), she pointed to noticing when we are in a defended or threatened state. That is when our ego feels the greatest need to protect our sense of identity.

In addition to the above of course, we each have biases that are unique to our mindset based on the culture we grew up in or the culture we work in.

Now, if you're like me, a discussion about these five biases may be unsettling to your stomach: *"How can it be that I have such little control in this world?" How can I be so wrong?" Let's just ignore this part of the book."*

Take a deep breath. Invite your Empathic Neural Network to activate. And know that you're not alone. We have created a checklist for you below that will help you ask these questions and also bring these to your team (so they don't think you're the only one confused or lacking in confidence).

Bias Checklist For Complex Situations

Actions	Why This Works
☑ Ask yourself "How can I be wrong?"	Helps you have an open mind for learning.
☑ Ask yourself "What am I missing?"	Helps you see more of the full picture.
☑ Ask yourself "Which other perspectives are missing?"	Helps you invite diverse perspectives.
☑ Use language like "My perspective, assumption, story is" rather than make your statements as facts.	Helps others know that you're open to learning from them.
☑ Get a team member to play devil's advocate.	Helps teams make better decisions.
☑ Ask yourself "How is this other person right?" or "How do they see the world?"	Helps you better understand others to influence and collaborate with them.
☑ Listen to learn, to empathize, to be moved.	Helps you learn, collaborate, and be creative.

Start to get comfortable using new language in your conversations that signal to yourself and others that you are open to new thinking, open to learning about new perspectives, and are willing to declare your assumptions and biases. In the world of unpredictability, behaviors that will serve are not expertise, but openness to learning (trust me, this comes from lots of experts!).

Accelerator 3: Meta-Learn

U.S. President Abraham Lincoln famously said, "The best way to predict the future is to create it". This is so relevant during times of disruption. In these times, we can't accurately predict the future, but we can participate in creating it through meta-learning. Meta-learning is the state of "being aware of and taking control of one's own learning". In the context of a disruption, meta-learning is becoming aware of and adapting your learning process to the situation at hand.

For Learning Agility, we train our minds to slow down to be in the present moment. We bring ourselves back to this moment to learn about what's happening now inside of us (neuro-state and mindset) and in our environment. We deepen our attention span to the now. We widen our view of what we notice in the landscape, both within and outside of us. We step in. We step back. We learn. We let go of the old. We bring in the new. It's an on-going loop that we practice in the present moment. Here's what that looks like and we even came up with an acronym for it.

The L.E.A.R.N. Practice ™

Listen into your internal state (what is my current neuro-emotional state?)

Eye the environment for what's happening now (what's the context I'm in?)

Aspire what would my best-self do in this situation?)

Run an experiment (take a small action toward what's important). This gives you a sense of agency and control and you learn from it.

Notice the results (what am I learning here from the experiment?)

The L.E.A.R.N. Practice™

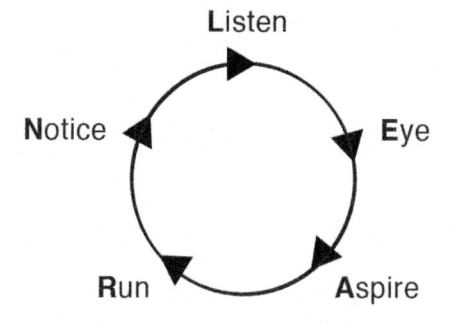

In disruptions, when we can't really predict the future, present moment learning and engaging in the system we're in helps us to learn more. In a less predictable situation, practice spending less energy planning and more on co-creating the emerging future. The more you bring this meta-learning mindset to the situation you have the more your brain will habitually learn to learn.

The L.E.A.R.N Practice ™ helps us grow by training our ability to be present to our inner state and our environment as each shift. We shift to our aspirational selves to experiment and act and be part of the emerging future. It brings our inner state to impact our environment and learning from our environment to connect with intuition and creativity. It's an on-going loop.

Mindfulness practice is a great way to train ourselves and deepen The L.E.A.R.N. Practice ™. It helps us to train our attention and focus. Our mind under stress can be like a nervous little puppy jumping from one activity to another. Training our mind is like training the puppy. We need patience, kindness, love, and lots of practice.

As we start to notice our ego impulses through mindfulness practice, we can ease into knowing that in this present moment, we are okay. We don't have to have all the answers and we ease into being okay with not being in control. We may not have control over our environment but we can influence it. We can move purposefully toward what matters and connect with others with shared values and a vision for a better world.

Steve Jobs was a practitioner of mindfulness. Jobs biographer Walter Isaacson quotes Jobs explaining this way of thinking:

> *"If you just sit and observe, you will see how restless your mind is. If you try to calm it, it only makes it worse, but over time it does calm, and when it does, there's room to hear more subtle things--that's when your intuition starts to blossom and you start to see things more clearly and be in the present more. Your mind just slows down, and you see a tremendous expanse in the moment. You see so much more than you could see before."*[25]

There are now thousands of studies on mindfulness and its positive impact on brain structure and functioning. It enhances attention, emotional regulation and creativity. Just five minutes of regular practice helps. MRI research shows that just within eight weeks, the size of the pre-frontal cortex (our thinking and reasoning brain) grows and the threat-scanning amygdala becomes smaller.[26] A side-effect of this medication for your brain is that you actually feel less stressed. Meditation is actually great medication for the brain!

In the context of a leader who is leading in disruption, mindfulness practice will help you calm your own nervous system (and keep it less susceptible to over-firing in response to threats). It will help you be more sensitive and compassionate with yourself and others in threat states. It will help you read situations more accurately and take a step back to notice what's actually happening. It will help you feel more connected to others, creating greater trust. It will help you be more creative and be open to new ideas and opportunities.

If you haven't tried it yet, please do. I have an entire course on mindfulness with five-minute exercises on LinkedIn Learning (it's been taken by over 250,000 people as of this writing). It has specific practices for dealing in challenging times, growing focus, and staying calm.

There are many tools to practice mindfulness including apps and many wonderful mindfulness teachers and websites. The perfect mindfulness practice is what works for you and is one that you will want to stick with.

Micro-Behaviors for Learning Agility

1. Listens to learn rather than to confirm what they already know
2. Questions and shares own assumptions and biases
3. Explores others' perspectives with curiosity
4. Experiments with new ways of doing things
5. Embraces failure as a learning opportunity
6. Steps back to understand context of the challenge

Questions for Reflection

1. Pick a problem you're trying to solve. In what area of the Cynefin Framework does it belong? What opens up when you apply the relevant questions to that problem?

2. What are the biases that most resonated for you that prevent you from learning?

Experiments to Try
1. Review the "Bias Checklist". Pick one action that resonates with you and practice it.
2. As a thought experiment, pick a belief you're open to challenging. Now take the opposite view. What do you see now?
3. In your next conversation, share your assumptions and biases and ask about others' assumptions. What opens up?
4. Pick an area where you'd like to try The L.E.A.R.N. Practice ™. Try it and reflect on what you learned.

Additional Information
1. To take a long stroll into the world of biases, this (https://medium.com/better-humans/cognitive-bias-cheat-sheet-55a472476b18) is a great resource.
2. LinkedIn Learning Mindfulness Practices for Work (https://www.linkedin.com/learning/mindfulness-practices/) course.
3. Podcast with Jennifer Garvey Berger (https://transformleaders.tv/jennifer-garvey-berger/) on brain biases & deep listening.

4
Trust Agility

The success of an intervention depends on the interior condition of the intervenor.
—Bill O'Brien, the late CEO of Hanover Insurance

Our workplaces and teams are now more diverse (multi-generational, global, virtual, across organizational boundaries) and fluid than ever. As a result of COVID-19, we're getting a taste of how networks of teams are coming together to solve problems quickly. They're operating outside of existing organizational hierarchy and bureaucratic structures. Many organizations are already experimenting with creating internal marketplaces of talent and skill sets. Cisco is creating its own gig economy for employees.[27]

COVID-19 is also helping us experiment with tapping into employees outside our organizations. For example, the national supermarket chain Kroger, temporarily borrowed furloughed employees for 30 days from Sysco Corporation, a wholesale food distributor to restaurants that has been hit hard by the coronavirus.[28]

For a deeper dive on how organizations and leaders need to adapt to the future of work, listen to my podcast with Ravin Jesuthasan at the end of this chapter.

Fluid teams are the workforce of the future and Trust Agility will be the currency of this workforce. Trust Agility is the ability to rapidly adapt yourself to meet people where they are and build trust with them. By doing this in your team, you speed up agility to change and energize people to make their best contributions in a disruptive environment.

It creates trusted cultures because people feel as if their managers genuinely care about them as individuals. Research from the company, *Great Places to Work,* shows that in high trust cultures people are nine times more likely to adapt to a new way of working.[29]

Trust Agility Challenges in Disruption

There are three primary challenges to Trust Agility in times of disruption.

1. Disruptions can cause prior trust issues to deepen if our stress behaviors arise. This is why we have to start first within ourselves in trusting others and to have conversations that repair broken trust. This requires a growth shift in our own ego.

2. Within an organizational context, disruptions cause restructuring. Any restructuring creates a 45 percent change in people's experience according to Great Places to Work research. There are many people who feel left behind in a change environment. People need even greater levels of trust during times of disruption because disruptions activate

threat state. Trust in a system creates psychological safety which allows for more creativity in the face of change. Though our instinct may be to first work on the "problem" that we're trying to solve, resist that instinct and spend time deepening the connection.

3. The third challenge in disruptions are that while people are looking for clarity and direction, there is often great ambiguity. This can cause leaders to disappear, provide false hope, or be overly confident in their expertise. This stems from a historical hierarchical mindset that leaders must have all the answers and disseminate solutions from the top.

In disruptions, we can tend to micro-manage decision-making or closely control and consolidate power because we ourselves are in a state of threat. This lowers signals of trust. Instead we need to give people a greater sense of autonomy and control as that actually lowers their threat level.

Accelerator 1: Trust First

Our own neuro-emotional state matters because it forms the basis for our trust behaviors. Our intent is not just understood by others, it actually creates changes in their blood chemistry.

Research done by Dr. Paul Zak looking at human cooperation shows that the neurochemical oxytocin plays a significant role in trust.[30] When we trust someone, we actually cause oxytocin to be released in their brains. High levels of oxytocin cause people to work harder to help the group achieve its goals. Zak's team developed a safe way to infuse synthetic oxytocin into living human brains. Their research showed that research participants willing to self-sacrifice to help others (even those very different from them) flourished.[31]

Dr. Zak then went to a number of businesses such as retailer Zappos.com and office designer Herman Miller. The leadership in these two companies as example agreed to let Zak draw blood and measure brain activity from their employees as they worked. He was able to confirm his lab findings that teams that cause an oxytocin release in each other were more productive and innovative. They enjoyed the tasks they were doing more than the participants of teams whose brains did not connect with their teammates.

Dr. Zak's next adventure was to test the role of oxytocin on teamwork in the rain forest in Papua New Guinea. With the help of an anthropologist, he conducted a study with the Malke people who are subsistence farmers living without electricity, plumbing or doctors. He took blood samples and measured oxytocin before and after a traditional dance that preceded group work. His findings showed that people moving in unison during the dance produced oxytocin.

Chapter 4 Trust Agility

What does this research relate to? We start with trusting first. And in case you're still not trusting the trust data, here is more data about why trusting first matters. When we experience release of oxytocin in our own blood stream, it actually serves to weaken connections in the fear hub of the brain. So, if your workplace had a bar serving oxytocin, you would be buying drinks for everyone!

In my work with executive coaching clients, most of us want the other person to take the first step. Instead, we have to actively confront our own "stories" and biases about other people. I recently used the Mind Story Map ™ with an executive coaching client who was struggling with a trust gap with her peer. She felt frustrated because he seemed to thwart her attempts to move the business forward. The tool helped her to pause her stories about him and the situation. It helped her to connect more deeply with the emotions she was having.

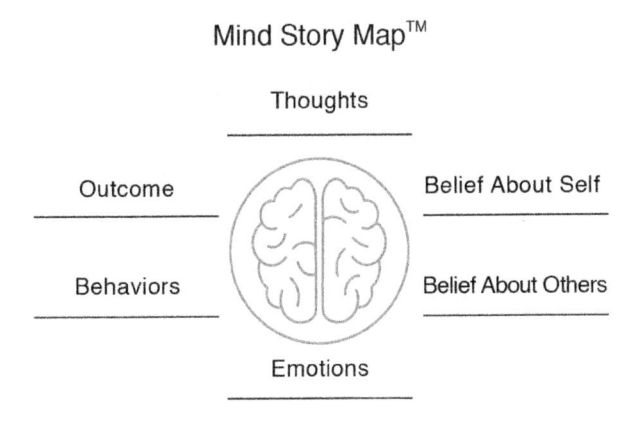

Mind Story Map™

Thoughts

Outcome   Belief About Self

Behaviors   Belief About Others

Emotions

As she connected with the emotion, she realized that underneath the frustration was deep hurt. The hurt stemmed from how he didn't trust her or have her back. They had had a strong working relationship in the past and she was confused about what had changed. I listened deeply to help her explore this hurt. Tears followed. When we bring compassion to our emotional state, it can help us to transcend our ego and drop into Empathic Neural States. As she opened up, she became more curious about how he saw this situation.

What would his Mind Story Map ™ look like? At the end of the exercise, she had determined that she wanted to have a different conversation with him, one where each could share their own "story". Listening deeply to each other's stories can give us the opportunity to question our biases about the other person and make a different choice. Of course, this choice cannot be forced.

Another great tool is one from the best-seller by the Arbinger Institute, *The Anatomy of Peace*. This tool helps us very simply see what box we may be in that erodes trust with others.[32]

As Arbinger Institute's book explains, when we have a relationship with others that is not fully trusting we are likely in one of four boxes: we see ourselves as better than others; we see ourselves as worse than others; we see ourselves as a victim of others' actions; or we want to be seen in a certain way by others. All of these states are normal for our ego, which is designed

The Trust First Accelerator

The Better-Than Box

View of Myself	View of Others
Superior	Inferior
Important	Incapable/Irrelevant
Virtuous/Right	False/Wrong

Feelings	View of World
Impatient	Competitive
Disdainful	Troubled
Indifferent	Needs Me

The Worse-Than Box

View of Myself	View of Others
Not as Good	Advantaged
Broken/Deficient	Privileged
Failed	Blessed

Feelings	View of World
Helpless	Hard/Difficult
Jealous/Bitter	Against Me
Depressed	Ignoring Me

The Must-Be-Seen Box

View of Myself	View of Others
Need to be well thought of	Judgmental
Fake	Threatening
	My audience

Feelings	View of World
Anxious/Afraid	Dangerous
Needy/Stressed	Watching
Overwhelmed	Judging Me

The I-Deserve Box

View of Myself	View of Others
Meritorious	Mistaken
Mistreated/Victim	Mistreating
Unappreciated	Ungrateful

Feelings	View of World
Entitled	Unfair
Deprived	Unjust
Resentful	Owes Me

Source: The Anatomy of Peace

to protect us. We often find ourselves in one of these four states, particularly when we're under stress or threat. Our work then is to notice which box we're in and step ourselves out of it so we can establish more authentic connection with others.

There are also great checklists to establish trust in the book *The Speed of Trust* by Stephen M. R. Covey.[33] These include extending trust first, demonstrating vulnerability, making things right, listening well, communicating transparently, confronting reality and trying our best to make and keep commitments.

Our actual ability to behave in these ways in a consistent manner is contingent upon our ability to come back to being present and centered and managing our own neurobiology first. It is also contingent upon the culture of the team that we're working within, for team cultures impact our own neurobiology, especially the behavior of the leaders of a team.

Accelerator 2: Deepen Connection

The empathy dialogue is to deepen trust and explore common ground. Interpersonal conflict often arises when we attribute our differences to differences in character or values between us and the other person. The empathy dialogue helps us to dig deeper to truly understand others. As we do this, we discover that others' views are created by experiences they have had that we are just beginning to understand.

We are in a rising epidemic of loneliness in the workplace. In the United States, even before the social distancing rules brought on by COVID-19, about 60 percent of Americans shared that they felt lonely, up significantly from the prior year.[34] In times of disruption, we find ourselves stretched and need even more support. As we learned earlier in this chapter, a sense of connection actually reduces our threat levels and enables us to better adapt to change. Thus, our ability

Chapter 4 Trust Agility

to create vulnerability-based trust with people is the support that helps them stretch, take risks, and grow.

As an executive coach to C-level leaders, I have the privilege and feel immensely grateful for the opportunity to create a safe space for these leaders to reveal their innermost fears, dreams, doubts, and triumphs. The kind of trust that is established in this connection helps them to stretch outside their comfort zone, to grow and feel supported. It's a cardinal element of the research done by Richard Boyatzis for his book *Helping People Change*. Anecdotally, the higher the place in the hierarchy oftentimes the lonelier the experience can be for an individual.

Vulnerability based trust in the workplace is the currency of agile teams. While we are technically not coaches for each other, I believe we can cultivate "coach-like" trusted partnerships with one another; and a place to start is to deepen our connection.

The trust we are talking about here is vulnerability-based trust. It is about establishing that you care for others' well-being. Our human brain evolved to intuit within just a few seconds whether someone could be trusted first and then to figure out whether they are useful or competent.[35] So today, we ask ourselves:

- Does this person have a benevolent intention toward me?
- Are they safe for me to open up to and share that I don't know the answers?

Wired for Disruption

this team going to judge me? Can I let them know that I failed?
- Can I let them know that I am not feeling heard?

Vulnerability-based trust is the foundation of team performance. In his best-selling book *The Five Dysfunctions of a Team,* Patrick Lencioni shares the pivotal connection between vulnerability-based trust and team performance and results.[36]

Working with lots of senior teams, I have seen firsthand how when we open up to share ourselves and our stories of what is meaningful for us, it helps to deepen connection. Storytelling has been influencing our behaviors and changing attitudes since the first cave paintings tens of thousands of years ago. It actually changes blood chemistry through shared connection because we are not just spectators in another's story. <u>We feel what they feel. It builds vulnerability-based trust and a sense of safety that helps teams be more agile.</u>[37] When I facilitate teams in this exercise, I always ask the leader of the team to go first. As the leader shares a personal vulnerable story, it creates a safe space for other to do so as well.

Here are three types of vulnerable stories that are useful to share:
- A meaningful or challenging experience when you were young.
- A story of when you were challenged and what you learned.

Chapter 4 Trust Agility

- A story of an unexpected change, how you handled it, and what you learned.

Other ways to deepen connection include <u>learning about other teammates' aspirations and challenges.</u> Starting with aspirations shifts the brain state to imagining about the future which is part of the Empathic Neural Network. Here is an <u>Empathy Dialogue Tool ™</u> that I have used with client teams in virtual settings. It helps to grow shared understanding and empathy.

The Empathy Dialogue Tool™

Aspirations	Strengths
1. **Aspirations:** If your work & life were ideal what would it be like in 5 years? 2. **Purpose:** How do you want to serve others that also inspires you? 3. **Values:** Who do you admire and why? Describe a meaningful experience growing up. What made this meaningful for you? What do you feel grateful for?	1. **Strengths:** Describe a time when you were performing at your peak. What strengths did you use? 2. **Energizers:** Describe a time you felt energized and inspired. What were you doing? Who were you being? What was your impact on others? 3. **Resilience:** Describe a time when you successfully faced a challenge. What did you learn?
Challenges	Perspectives
1. What makes you upset or frustrated? 2. What are the obstacles to your ideal work and life in 5 years?	1. What's your perspective on ____ (pick a common topic of interest). 2. What experiences have shaped this perspective? 3. What if we ____ (co-create question)
Bias Check (For Yourself Only)	Feedback
What biases can filter how I'm seeing this person?	How can I be even more effective as a leader to serve you?

The last part of the dialogue includes getting feedback from others about how we can be effective for them. This is part of Marshall Goldsmith's Stakeholder-Centered Coaching model. It helps us get into a mindset of humility and curiosity, shifting us out of protective ego-centered mindsets.

Of course, if trust is broken, we need to address that broken trust first. From personal experience and working with clients (as in the story above), this can be hard because it requires transcending of our ego to have compassion for our own hurt or anger and that of the other person.

A word here about our in-group bias (our preference for people like us). In times of disruption, that bias is likely operating on overdrive. In these times, it's especially important to reach out to the voices that are less heard by us. Leaders must make a special effort to hear the minority voices and help them feel included. This accelerator to deepen connection is especially important for finding creative solutions in disruptions and to engage everyone in the dialogue. As we listen and share, we find that our common ground moves. As we develop connection with others, we discover common aspirations, values, challenges, needs, and goals. This helps us to create real trust with teammates. It helps us broaden our circle of concern toward them, to genuinely care for them as human beings.

Chapter 4 Trust Agility

[Handwritten note: USE: INFLUENCING TOOL]

Common Ground

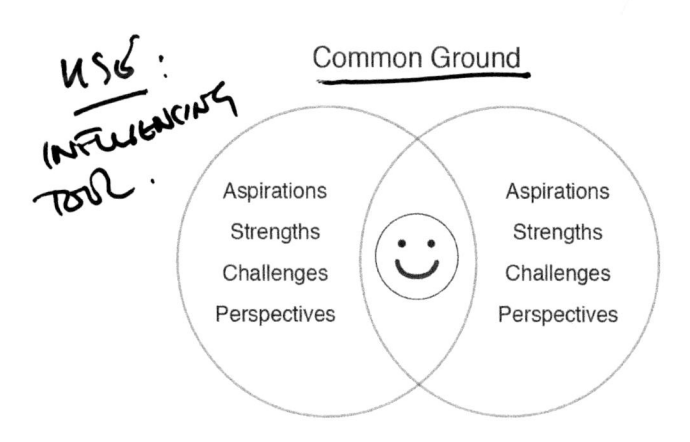

- Aspirations
- Strengths
- Challenges
- Perspectives

- Aspirations
- Strengths
- Challenges
- Perspectives

An essential contributor to trust (and agility as a whole) is to train ourselves to listen well. Listening well—and indeed listening at Level 4—changes us. We become open to being moved by and influenced by others. We listen to truly learn from others, to connect with them.

As we listen without judgment, the Empathic Neural Networks in both bodies are activated and we find ourselves caring for the other, fascinated by how they make sense of their world, and feeling compassion for their challenges. We let go of the ego paradigm of "power over" someone in favor of our collective "power-to" in order to create an emerging future that we all believe in.

As you listen to the end of our podcast with Jennifer Garvey Berger, we come to the conclusion that listening deeply is really an act of love, a gift we offer to others that comes back to us. In her book, *Love 2.0*, Dr. Barbara Fredrickson shares data about how these micro-moments of connection with others boost immunity and well-being for each participant.[38]

Four Levels of Listening

Level	Intent	Focus On	Sounds Like
Level 1 Hearing	To contribute what I already know	**My Competence** What I already know, how I'm right, how to fix their problem	"I know, I get it..." "I was right..." "You should..."
Level 2 Seeing	To find new data	**Their Content** Words, numbers, facts past experience (external realities)	"I didn't know that!" "Wow, look at that!"
Level 3 Feeling	To relate	**Their Concerns** Tone, body language, facial expressions, rate/volume of speech, energy (internal realities)	"You seem..." "How do you feel about..."
Level 4 Intuiting	To learn, grow, and be steered to new solutions	**Larger Context** Includes the ecosystem including me, interdependencies	"I didn't realize..." "I learned..." "How about we..."

Accelerator 3: Communicate Shared Purpose & Empathy

In times of disruption, when people are looking for certainty, we may not be able to give the specific information that will help others feel safe. However, clarity is the next best thing to certainty and empathy is what's most important. Reminding people of shared purpose and identity is critical because it activates the Empathic

Neural Networks in our brain. Even though we don't know what the exact future will be like, we point them to our current shared reality, purpose and values. If a common purpose doesn't yet exist, we co-create it.[39]

A great example of pointing to shared purpose was Microsoft CEO Satya Nadella's March 21 note to employees titled "Coming together to Combat COVID-19).[40] There are seven key elements of his note that every leader can emulate:

- First, he reminded employees of Microsoft's mission: "Empower every person and every organization on the planet to achieve more".
- Second, he grounded everyone in the reality of what is happening.
- Third, he expressed gratitude and pointed people to their contributions: "I want to share my deepest thanks to each of you for the creative and collaborative ways you have stepped up to support our company and our customers during this crisis. It's times like this that remind us that each of us has something to contribute and the importance of coming together as a community." When we thank people for the adaptive behaviors, we observe we lower threat level and we build their identity as being resilient. It helps them to have confidence in themselves and actually move toward greater resilience.
- Fourth, he demonstrated empathy by talking

about the employees concerns first: "Please know that the senior leadership team and I are thinking about you and prioritizing the health and safety of you and your families first and foremost."
- Fifth, he established authentic and vulnerable connection: "I myself am learning, as I'm sharing a home office with my two teenage daughters and juggling between their eLearning schedules and my Teams meetings."
- Sixth, he reminded people of values that are important in this time, care for employees and customers: "There is no playbook for this and having that deep empathy and understanding for each other's situations is needed now more than ever. We're providing critical infrastructure for the communities where we operate, and they are counting on us.".
- Lastly, he gave employees something to feel proud about how Microsoft is working across public and private domains to make an impact.

One might look at Microsoft and think, sure, that was an easy message. Microsoft is not impacted in the same way as other companies.

Let's look at Marriott CEO Arne Sorenson's response.[41] He is in an industry that is devastated by COVID-19. That same day in March 2020, in his message to employees (video link is at the end of this

Chapter 4 Trust Agility

chapter), he started by grounding people in the facts: "Our business is running 75 percent below normal. Hundreds of hotels will need to close until demand returns". He shared the Management's response plan starting with the non-employee related cuts: Marketing, initiatives, CEO salary and executive team salaries.

His visible emotion at having to cut employment demonstrated his empathy: "I can tell you that I have never had a more difficult moment than this one. There is simply nothing worse than having to tell highly valued associates that their roles are being impacted by events completely outside their control". His emotion is visible as he says this. He ends with a message of hope and determination to see the company through this time.

Micro-Behaviors for Trust Agility

1. Helps others feel understood and cared for.
2. Creates an environment of trust.
3. Demonstrates respect for others.
4. Communicates with transparency.
5. Is the first to makes things right when there is a trust gap in relationships.
6. Creates clarity even if there is no certainty.
7. Reminds people of shared purpose and values.

Questions for Reflection
1. Reflect on the people with whom you have high trust. What does that enable?
2. Reflect on the people with whom you have low trust. What are the costs?
3. For those with whom trust is compromised, look at the "Ego States Affect Trust" framework. What box have you unconsciously placed yourself in?

Experiments to Try
1. Download the Empathy Dialogue Tool ™ (https://transformleaders.tv/wiredfordisruption/) from our website. Use the tool to have a dialogue with a trusted friend or colleague. Notice how it feels to experience empathy.
2. Use the Empathy Dialogue Tool ™ with someone you're curious to get to know better. Use Level 3 listening skills. What did you learn?
3. Now ask someone with whom you have a somewhat difficult relationship, to see if they would be willing to use the Empathy Dialogue Tool ™ to connect. What did you learn?

Additional Resources
1. Podcast – Ravin Jesuthasan – The Future of Work (https://transformleaders.tv/ravin-jesuthasan/)

Chapter 4 Trust Agility

2. Podcast with Charlene Li – The Disruption Mindset (https://transformleaders.tv/charene-li/)
3. Download Agility Accelerators (https://transformleaders.tv/wiredfordisruption/) from website (available by May 28, 2020)
4. Marriott CEO (https://www.youtube.com/watch?v=SprFgoU6aO0) Video Link

5

Stakeholder Agility

What's really needed is a deeper shift in consciousness so that we begin to care and act, not just for ourselves and other stakeholders but in the interests of the entire ecosystem.
—Otto Scharmer, MIT Senior Lecturer, Founding Chair, Presencing Institute

"I just can't get him to see that he needs to restructure his organization!", Jane the Chief Marketing Officer (CMO) exclaimed in frustration. "His people aren't responding to what our customers need now. They aren't even asking the right questions!" Jane had come out of a series of meetings with customers and was complaining about how her peer Joe, the Head of Sales, just could not see how "incompetent" his people were.

Jane had tried to convince Joe to see her point of view and it was falling on deaf ears. This scene plays out again and again in many organizations. We try to influence others to see the world as we see it. But we're looking from two different looking glasses. We need to get curious about the looking glass we're looking from and that of the other person.

Chapter 5 Stakeholder Agility 97

As we get to higher levels in the hierarchy, there are even more stakeholders who we need to influence. This makes these jobs even more complex because human behavior is not highly predictable. CEOs and C-level leaders I work with need to influence their boards, competing voices of peers and industry ecosystems. In disruptions, the stakes are even higher because change is happening quickly, we all want more control than we have and time is of the essence. Many leaders confess to being frustrated by the behaviors and decisions of their peers because they have not yet learned Stakeholder Agility.

What is Stakeholder Agility?

Stakeholder Agility is the ability to flex to see, understand, and care for the needs of multiple groups within the ecosystem and to care for the ecosystem as a whole. It requires being able to see multiple perspectives, notice the looking glass we ourselves see from and accept the looking glass others see from. Stakeholders include customers, shareholders, employees, suppliers, governments, communities where we do business, partners, even activists who challenge us.

The reason Stakeholder Agility is important in disruptions is that disruptions are a great opportunity to create something new. Behaviors and attitudes may be changing as technology changes. Novel approaches become available to solving problems. Or as in the case of COVID-19 or even climate change, we need to solve critical ecosystem issues with others who are part of the ecosystem.

As we evolve, I believe more and more of us are seeing the planet as a key stakeholder in our individual and collective decision-making. We're increasingly solving problems that are complex and involve aligning and leveraging multiple stakeholders with different needs across an organization or system. This is also where big opportunities are found, common purpose moved and big threats avoided.

At a macro level, human beings are increasingly faced with solving problems that require shared ownership and action. Disruptive challenges such as climate action, COVID-19 response, turbulence in interconnected financial markets, strained supply chains, and drained economies require Stakeholder Agility. Within an organization, we must increasingly learn to manage the tension of competing stakeholder needs, and within a team or family, manage the tension of competing needs. The key to managing these tensions is to engage in a purpose-oriented, curiosity-fueled, trust-building way with the system as a whole.

In my podcast interview with Harry Kraemer, former CEO of Baxter International, he shared how he made a tough decision having to recall one of their pharmaceutical drugs and write off millions of dollars. In my own experience of having to lead through the

Chapter 5 Stakeholder Agility

disruption of a recall in my role as a region president, the pressure of managing multiple voices is intense. This is where a practice of self-reflection that helps us step back to see ourselves, others, and the ecosystem more clearly is critical.

Many companies during the COVID-19 pandemic have stepped up to lead ecosystems. Pharmaceutical companies, traditionally tough competitors, are collaborating to find a vaccine. Albert Bourla, CEO of the pharmaceutical company Pfizer Corporation talked with Fortune: "This is not business as usual. ROI should not drive our decisions at all", he said, "I always say to my people, the other pharmaceutical companies are not the competition. The competition is the disease."

This is even more relevant today. We are collaborating like never before." He talked about how his people have been enlivened by shared purpose. He believes, the company after the crisis "will be at the forefront of leading the way in demonstrating contribution to society." He was one of the 181 CEOs in August 2019 who signed onto the Business Roundtable's statement calling for a greater focus on companies' contribution to stakeholders beyond just shareholders.[42]

Bourla added, "It was clear that our business model was not sustainable if we don't create value for patients and value for society."[43]

Companies like Danone continue to operate with over 60 percent of their 100,000 employees operating factories and distributing products. Danone has enjoyed its place Fortune's Change the World list for its focus on social benefits, and is working to convert the entire company to B-Corporation status over the next decade. B-Corporations are a new kind of company that works to balance purpose and profit across a range of stakeholders.[44] *Fortune* is actually gathering a list of greatest leaders in the crisis which can be found here.[45]

Even prior to COVID-19, there was already developing a move toward multi-stakeholder capitalism. The Business Roundtable declared the purpose of a corporation to deliver value to customers, invest in employees, deal fairly with suppliers, support communities, and generate long-term value for shareholders.

In January 2020, Larry Fink, the CEO of Black Rock, the largest global investment manager stunned CEOs with his letter to shareholders talking about the urgency of focusing on sustainability. In his letter to CEOs, Fink asked them to consider climate risk as investment risk.[46] He challenged the financial market's ecosystem to find ways to align shareholder returns with sustainability goals.

In my view, the COVID-19 pandemic will have taught us an urgent lesson—that we're far more connected and interdependent than we thought before. What is taking climate change activists a long time to accomplish, COVID-19 is doing with great urgency. It is creating a mindset shift to realize that our collective

Chapter 5 Stakeholder Agility

actions matter and we must learn to lead with Stakeholder Agility to ensure our collective future.

While these are much-needed mindset shifts and actions for a sustainable interdependent world, it creates significant leadership tension. All of our current systems—how we account for our balance sheets and profit and loss, how we value companies, and CEO incentives—are mostly set up for managing to shareholder returns. There will be a need for significant disruption in these areas if we are to create a more sustainable world.

There is also a significant shift needed in Stakeholder Agility. We need leaders who can manage the complex challenge of meeting competing stakeholder needs. For example, in the COVID-19 pandemic situation, CEOs have had to manage the tension of protecting employees' salaries or employment status against staying afloat financially. For leaders at global airlines and hospitality businesses, these were tough decisions and the accelerators identified below are based on case studies of how these leaders led within the tension.

At a micro-level, each of us as leaders are managing these tensions, whether it is managing the competing needs of investing in existing business versus the innovative technology that will disrupt it, or investing in existing versus emerging customers.

Stakeholder Challenges in Disruption

Here are three challenges of managing stakeholders during times of disruption.

1. In disruptions new stakeholders emerge, whether it is a new customer or new partner opportunity. With normal biases we might not even notice these emerging opportunities or write them off because we are only talking to the people we know and like. The first thing to do is to map out our emerging ecosystem to understand what's here including the far reaches of the ecosystem.

2. The problems we are solving in disruptive environments require us to influence people that may have different priorities and needs than we do. Under stress our self-protective ego kicks in and our focus narrows. Our first impulse may be to see the world from the lens of personal or tribal interest and find safety in prioritizing our needs. Yet, we need others to move our agenda forward. Therefore, we need deeper listening to explore others' needs.

3. As we widen engagement with others, we face the challenge of serving multiple stakeholders with competing needs. This requires a completely new level of listening (listening at Level 4), holding multiple perspectives, and facilitation skills because unlike the people we work with in our hierarchy, incentives may not be aligned.

Stakeholder Accelerators

There are three accelerators that are useful in times of disruption.

1. First, we widen the lens to see the entire system we're operating in. Who are all the players in our "system" that are influencing this issue or working on the same problem we're working on? While our neurobiology may cause us to contract our peripheral vision, we can choose to step back and expand it and use the trust tools we've been practicing with.

2. Second, we need to use our Empathy Dialogue Tool ™ to understand the needs of players in the eco-system. What are the issues important to these stakeholders and how do we listen even deeper?

3. Third, as we listen more deeply, we open up new creative solutions that were not available because we broaden our circle of concern to the bigger ecosystem within which we exist.

Accelerator 1: Widen the View of the Ecosystem

The definition of an ecosystem is a biological community of interacting organisms and their physical environment. In our disruption context, it is the network of different people and organizations that are connected, influencing, and influenced by the disruption.

We humans of course have always been part of an ecosystem on our planet. We influence and are influenced by the biome of the planet, the community of plants and animals that share common characteristics. We are also part of ecosystems in our family, organizations, and nations.

The planet we are part of has systems that are hierarchical (e.g. lions, apes, bees, most current organization structures) as well as egalitarian (migrating birds, ants, Muriqui monkeys, just to name a few.)

Nature encodes behavior to prioritize survival of the species. For situations of collective survival, we too must adapt mindset from an "ego-system" focused entirely on the well-being of oneself (whether that is an individual, a team, a tribe, a nation, the human race) to an ecosystem that emphasizes the well-being of the whole.

Most of us think of ourselves at the top of (or the most important part) of an ecosystem. That is part of our ego-focused thinking that is often exacerbated when we get into threat mode. We watch out for ourselves and our tribe to fight the common enemy.

Ego vs. Ecosystem

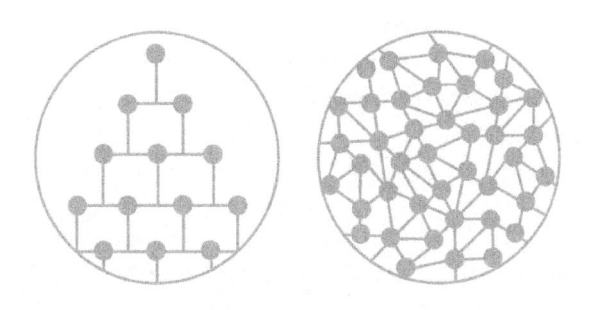

In his book *Leading from the Emerging Future*, Otto Scharmer lays out the way to move from our ego mindset to a more sustainable ecosystem mindset.[47] Of course, organizations don't shift mindset. It's the humans, one leader at a time, that lead the way.

In my view, the first place to start is to widen the lens, to map out your ecosystem, and to engage with curiosity using the Empathy Dialogue ™ tool.

Ecoystem Map

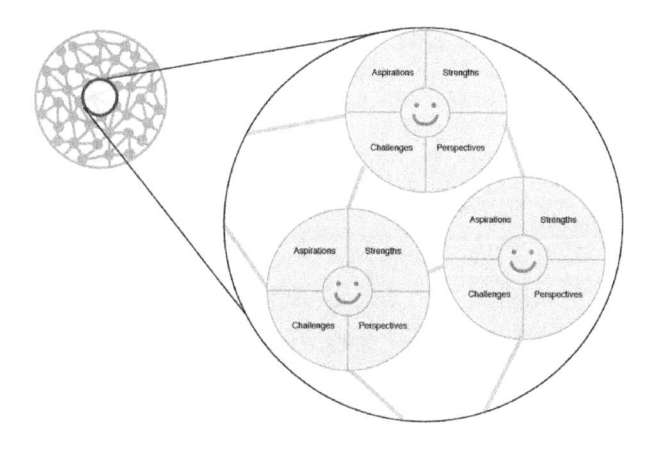

Accelerator 2: Listen Well

As we open up to our eco-system, we need to add a new level of listening. We use Level 4 listening to understand and connect with what matters to you and to others in the system.

Four Levels of Listening

Level	Intent	Focus On	Sounds Like
Level 1 Hearing	To contribute what I already know	**My Competence** What I already know, how I'm right, how to fix their problem	"I know, I get it..." "I was right..." "You should..."
Level 2 Seeing	To find new data	**Their Content** Words, numbers, facts past experience (external realities)	"I didn't know that!" "Wow, look at that!"
Level 3 Feeling	To relate	**Their Concerns** Tone, body language, facial expressions, rate/volume of speech, energy (internal realities)	"You seem..." "How do you feel about..."
Level 4 Intuiting	To learn, grow, and be steered to new solutions	**Larger Context** Includes the ecosystem including me, interdependencies	"I didn't realize..." "I learned..." "How about we..."

As we build trusted caring relationships in an ecosystem, it becomes possible to discover what's important to others, discover their aspirations, and find common ground. This shared reality and vision is way to create more adaptiveness within others and the system as a whole.

This is not just a shift in mind, it is a shift in heart. We find a way to see ourselves in the other, to step into their shoes and feel their challenges. We find a way to let go of our ego temptation to put ourselves first and put the whole first. This is tougher in western societies many of which prioritize individualism over the collective.

Many Asian cultures place the needs of the collective above that of the individual. In the case of COVID-19 as example, countries like Singapore and South Korea were able to flatten the curve quickly while Italy and Spain suffered many losses.

In the Empathy Dialogue ™ we engage in deeper listening. We open ourselves up to listening to learn. We open ourselves up to listening to be influenced and moved by the other person. We open ourselves up to changing our own point of view and truly stepping into another person's shoes to see and feel the world from their perspective.

From this space of listening, concern, and empathy, new solutions can be co-created. To develop genuine caring for others in the ecosystem is a journey in growth itself. It has been said that "the longest journey we take is from the head to the heart".

Accelerator 3: Facilitate Tensions

Johann Wolfgang von Goethe, a German writer and statesman, once called conversation "the most sublime of experiences". As we engage and build trusted partnerships in our ecosystem and looked for shared purpose, we are able to have facilitative dialogues with people where we are able to explore our own point of view, hold their point of view, and together come up with new solutions to the problem.

These solutions cannot emerge from a place of ego. They require Level 4 listening. We resist the temptation to believe that our point of view is the whole truth about a situation. We let go of our bias for the simple story. We let in that another's point of view is as important and valid to them as ours is to us. We have to shift mindsets of "win" or "lose" to care for something bigger than ourselves.

It requires a genuine care and concern for the other person and a loosening of our view of ourselves as the most important in our ecosystem. It requires we care collectively for something bigger than ourselves, a bigger purpose that wants to be expressed.

Questions for Reflection

1. What ecosystems are you part of in your personal and professional life?

2. What ego habits may get in the way of collaborating within your ecosystem?

3. What is an ecosystem that you are inspired to influence?

Experiments to Try

1. Draw out your stakeholder ecosystem for a workplace initiative. Download the Empathy Dialogue Tool from our website to identify information gaps you may have about the stakeholders.

2. Have an exploratory conversation with a stakeholder to connect with them and understand their aspirations and challenges and share yours. Listen

at Level 4.

3. As you learn more about your stakeholders, what new opportunities and solutions open up?

Micro-Behaviors for Stakeholder Agility

1. Steps back to understand the interconnections in an ecosystem.

2. Engages with a diverse set of stakeholders.

3. Demonstrates curiosity to know the aspirations and challenges of stakeholders.

4. Listens deeply and practices empathy for stakeholder concerns and needs.

5. Co-creates opportunities and solutions with others.

Additional Resources:

1. Podcast with Otto Scharmer (https://transformleaders.tv/otto-scharmer/) – leading with an ecosystem mindset and his resources (https://www.presencing.org/gaia).

2. Podcast with Harry Kraemer (https://transformleaders.tv/harry-kraemer/) – Former CEO Baxter International Inc.

3. Example of Haier's use of business ecosystems (https:/corporate-rebels.com/why-haier-introduced-ecosystems-and-how-they-work).

6
Growth Agility

No problem can be solved with the same level of consciousness that created it.
—Albert Einstein

In this decade, every single human being will be confronted with having to adjust to a world that is rapidly changing. While Artificial intelligence (AI) will augment people's work, offering them expertise and assistance, many jobs currently being performed by humans will be accomplished with AI and robots. Yet, new jobs will be created that require higher digital skills as well as human skills such empathy, creativity, collaboration and change management. Growth Agility is our ability to grow ourselves and others in such high-change and disruptive environments through pivotal conversations and experiments.

Leading a hybrid and fluid workforce of AI-enabled humans and robots will require Growth Agility. Leaders will need to manage the tsunami of shifts in skill sets with a balance of empathy and sense of urgency. Our experience teaches us that most digital transformations don't meet goals because we are not yet adept at helping humans adapt to change.

Chapter 6 Growth Agility

Changing mindsets and behaviors are hard because of our neurobiology. That is why our first agility is Neuro-Emotional Agility.

All forward-thinking organizations are working to upskill and reskill people. Forward thinking governments such Singapore and Denmark are creating public-private partnerships to upskill and reskill their citizens. In January 2020, the World Economic Forum announced a manifesto to reskill and upskill one billion people by 2030.[48] In my view, this work is even more urgent now.

While this reskilling work is necessary, it is not sufficient. Even with free education available now more than ever, it still requires human beings to be motivated to learn.

We need leaders at all levels in organizations who have the passion, humility and curiosity to grow themselves and others. This is especially important as decision-making gets distributed and we move to flatter hierarchies. Our teams need to become agile at growing together. I believe one of the highest purposes of any team or organization is to grow the people within the team.

To drive Growth Agility, we need a major shift in mindset in who a leader is and what a leader does. We need to expand our thinking from leader-as-expert with all the answers to leader-as-energizer of teams, leader-as-facilitator of co-creative dialogues, leader as someone who reminds people of the purpose and values of the organization, and leader as someone who grows agility in others.

To drive Growth Agility, we also need a shift in incentives. Here's a thought experiment: What if CEOs were rewarded disproportionately for the quality of talent they attracted and developed rather than their short-term results? What if we had a metric for valuing the collective potential of the people in our organization? What if we were able to book this metric as an asset rather than people costs as expenses?

What if investors started to value Environmental, Social, and Governance (ESG) metrics as much as financial returns? What if the CEO is coached by someone deeper in the organization who had a completely different perspective? What if there was a multiplier in a CEO's compensation based on an organizational health metric rather than just a financial metric? What if we redefined our highest purpose as leaders to grow the potential of all in our system (including ourselves)?

I imagine a world where this is possible, and I believe this work is being started by many leaders around the world as we move toward triple bottom line conversations.[49] This requires a mindset shift in the consciousness of leaders to one of caring for the whole over the needs of the few.

This evolution is not simply a nice thought or

dream state. It is necessary for solving the urgent and meaningful issues of our time. Our culture, our structures, and our problems can only be solved with a new level of thinking, which is what Albert Einstein's epigraph at the beginning of this chapter suggests. We need leaders who have evolved their level of consciousness.

Challenges to Growth Agility in Disruption

There are three primary challenges to Growth Agility in these times. First, we need to start by being humble and hungry enough to recognize the growth potential in ourselves. We need to learn how to grow by doing experiments. Second, we need to learn how to expand our focus and skills from solving problems to growing the capacity in others to learn and adapt. Third, in disruptive environments, we need to shift our mindsets from success and failure to learning.

We become hyper-focused on the threat rather than take a step back to find the opportunities in disruptions. We over-focus on success and failure in complex situations. This creates a fear-of-failure culture which prevents taking calculated risks and learning from them.

Growth Agility Accelerators

To get serious about developing people, we need to start with several paradigm shifts. We also need to help people learn new skills. And if we're going to stretch to grow ourselves, we need to reward experiments and learning, as outlined in the Accelerators below.

Accelerator 1: Grow Yourself First

In development as in trust, we start with ourselves first.

A disruptive new world requires a new way to develop ourselves. Today, leaders in many organizations create annual development plans after performance review cycles are complete. Many of these have skill-based courses to take, and success is defined as completing the course. Many learning and development organizations have speakers for conferences. That's great for new knowledge and motivation, but it is my belief that nothing changes until we change first.

The new kind of development that many leading organizations are engaging in is learning by doing. A leader creates short, safe-to-fail experiments where people grow from the experiment rather than a long list of annual development goals and plans.

The first place to start is for each of us to map out growth areas important for us to be effective. We then find collaborators who will help us with our learning experiment and give feedback. This can be done in the context of an organization or within a group of people you interact with who are your stakeholders. Asking for help itself is a practice that will help you grow.

My recommendation is to start with a desired future outcome and map backwards to the changes that are required within you to achieve that outcome. CEO coach and leadership guru Marshall Goldsmith asks you to pick one area to focus on at a time.

A tool that I use with my executive coaching clients is the Experiment-To-Grow ™ tool. We start with the desired result that is important. For example, remember Jane the CMO from Chapter 5 who is trying to get the head of sales to restructure his organization and upgrade talent? As we employed the Experiment-To-Grow Tool ™, Jane came to the realization that the results she was currently getting (i.e. nothing) were based on her mindset that her peer was completely out of touch with client needs and being overly loyal to his people.

As she got curious, she realized when she tried to engage with him that her body language and neuro-emotional state were in a guarded state. She decided to reframe the results she wanted to achieve. Rather than trying to get him to restructure his group, she decided to learn how to better influence him. She chose to create a safe-to-fail experiment to listen even more deeply in order to understand how *he* saw the world. Here's a diagram of the Experiment-To-Grow ™ tool.

Experiment-To-Grow Tool™

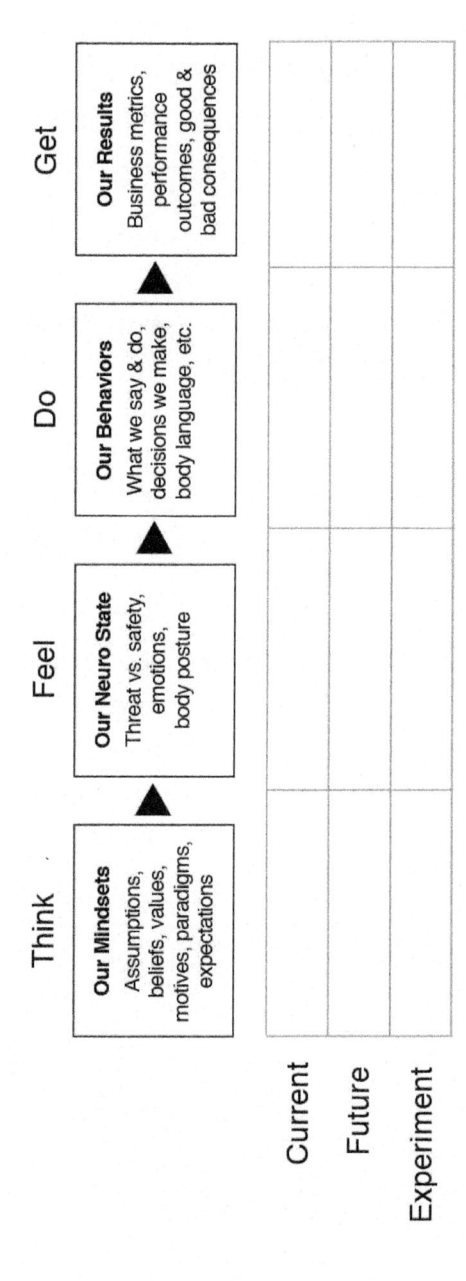

Think — **Our Mindsets**: Assumptions, beliefs, values, motives, paradigms, expectations

Feel — **Our Neuro State**: Threat vs. safety, emotions, body posture

Do — **Our Behaviors**: What we say & do, decisions we make, body language, etc.

Get — **Our Results**: Business metrics, performance outcomes, good & bad consequences

	Think	Feel	Do	Get
Current				
Future				
Experiment				

As she practiced deeper listening and saw what was important to him, it became easier to collaborate with him. He started to seek out her perspective as well on issues.

Accelerator 2: Ask Different Questions

A new competitor enters the market or a new technology is introduced making a company's product line obsolete. Disruptions create a sense of panic because the boss and the board want the defensive plan. In actuality, market shifts take time. It is the hierarchy-driven demands we put on ourselves that create panic. I've lived through (and truth be told, driven) many of these demands in my time in corporate America.

Time becomes even more scarce and we rush to solve the problem. We feel we don't have the time to have that coaching conversation. In disruption situations, we can tend to want to jump in and tell people what to do. However, the danger in this is that since there is often no "best practice" solution in a Complicated or Complex area in the Cynefin Framework, and a single person's perspective is limited, this approach may be sub-optimal.

Here is the difference between these two types of conversations. Think back to your last conversations with someone. Were you solving their problem or helping them learn?

As you'll notice from the chart on the next page, the mindset of the leader in a Growth Agility conversation is quite different than the mindset of the leader that focuses on solving the problem.

Growth Agility Conversation

Coaching Conversation	Useful Questions
Help person notice their neuro-state	- What's here? - Here's the body language I'm noticing.
Help the person explore their context	- What domain is this challenge in? - What does success look like?
Help the person explore their mindset or perspective	- How are you seeing this? - What biases may be present? - What are other ways to look at this?
Help the person grow confidence and commitment	- What strengths can you bring to this situation? - What values or purpose can be expressed?
Help a person influence their ecosystem & stakeholders	- Who is in your ecosystem? - What matters to them?

What the leader is aware of and pays attention to is very different. That mindset makes all the difference. Not only are new and different solutions created, but the team is more engaged in implementing those solutions, and people have a sense of shared pride and contribution. It's a shift of employee experience.

Accelerator 3: Reward Experiments & Learning

One of the biggest barriers to growth in disruptive times is fear. Our minds are trained to scan for threat and a failure is a major threat to ego and sense of belonging ("will they judge me?") and to paychecks. This prevents us from stepping outside our comfort zone to try something new. Trying something new is exactly what helps us learn. We have to deliberately change the conversation on failure – individually and institutionally.

Many organizations and leaders are comfortable in the "Obvious" and "Complicated" areas of the Cynefin Framework. We habitually turn to look for "best practice" or experts and cultures reward success and punish failure. In the "Complex" part of the framework, experiments are how we learn. It's how emerging practice is created. Leaders need to role-model creating safe-to-fail experiments to help learning happen.

Teams need to get comfortable setting up and learning from these experiments. A safe-to-fail experiment is one where we try something for the purpose of learning. Success is learning something. We shift our focus from that of an outcome to that of learning.

Failure vs. Learning

Failure Conversation	Learning Conversation
Intent is to fix the issue, find someone to blame.	Intent is to help the person learn.
Underlying mindset: Having a failure means someone is a failure.	Underlying mindset: A failure is an opportunity to learn what doesn't work. This helps us find what could work.
In obvious & predictable situations competency is easier to discern.	In complex situations, this mindset encourages a culture of experimentation and learning.
Questions: - Who's responsible? - How to hold them accountable?	Questions: - What did we learn? - What new experiment can we try?

When the focus is on an outcome, we tend to fall into failure conversation spirals that reduce experiments.

From the most urgent problem you're faced with today to the grand collective challenges of our planet, I ask you one simple question: "What new possibilities would be available if you shifted your consciousness?" We need to shift our collective consciousness toward a higher purpose of growing ourselves and others.

I leave you with a quote from George Bernard Shaw:

> *"This is the true joy in life, the being used for a purpose you consider a mighty one, the being a force of nature, rather than a feverish, selfish clod of ailments and grievances complaining that the world will not devote itself to making you happy".*

Micro-Behaviors for Growth Agility
1. Takes accountability to grow themselves.
2. Coaches others to help them grow.
3. Asks good questions to help others come up with solutions.
4. Rewards experimentation and learning.
5. Understands the difference between solving problems for others, feedback, and coaching.

Questions for Reflection
1. What is an area of your own growth that will serve you?
2. What are mindsets or beliefs can get in the way

of you coaching others?
3. What mindsets or beliefs do you have about failure?

Experiments
1. Create an experiment for the growth area you identified above. Discuss your experiment with a trusted colleague and see if they have any input. Conduct the experiment. What did you learn?
2. Pick a question from one of the charts above that you want to practice asking more frequently to grow others.

Additional Resources
1. Podcast with Bill Joiner: How To Grow (https://transformleaders.tv/bill-joiner/)
2. Podcast with Jimmy Parker on innovative approaches to grow at The Home Depot (https://transformleaders.tv/jimmy-parker/)
3. Podcast with Garry Ridge, CEO WD-40 about how CEOs create growth cultures (https://transformleaders.tv/garry-ridge/)
4. Podcast with Raj Sisodia about conscious capitalism and The Healing Organization. (https://transformleaders.tv/raj-sisodia/)
5. Michael Bungay Stanier's book *The Coaching Habit*
4. Hubspot (#1 Best Place to Work on Glassdoor) Culture Code[50]

Epilogue
My Hope for Our World

Our world has many tough problems that need solving. I believe many of us have a deep yearning to be an agent of positive change – a change that matters to us. How do we connect the needs of our world with the enormous potential of the people in it?

I believe the work starts inside each of us. We slow down to notice what matters. We connect with our experience to find the stories that move us and give rise to purpose. We connect with others for whom this purpose is resonant. We learn to be agile so we can be empowered agents for good and create a better world in this decade.

I imagine a world where we have emerged from the pandemic and its after-effects more connected to ourselves and others, more creative and more agile. I imagine us taking down the remnants of old systems and structures that no longer serve us. I imagine that we have found access to the switches that move us from threat and ego states to creative, caring, curious and connected states.

How we emerge is in each of our hands and in our practice. You are already wired to be agile in disruption. Now more than ever, you have a voice. It matters. Take the first step.

If you would like to be part of this community of change makers who are willing to grow to be a force for good in times of disruption, join our community at www.transformleaders.tv (http://www.transformleaders.tv/).

Let's together re-imagine what it is to be a leader in this brave new world we are creating.

Want to Learn More?

Visit http://www.TransformLeaders.tv/WiredForDisruption to download tools and templates.

Executive Coaching: Henna Inam works with mission-focused C-level leaders and our team can work with leaders through out your organization.

Speaking: Arrange for a keynote or workshop with Henna Inam. What differentiates Henna as a speaker is that her workshops are interactive and experiential. Each leader walks away with learning customized to their most pressing goals and challenges.

Agility Accelerator Lab: Mastermind groups for your team and organization

Agility Quiz: Take the *Wired for Disruption* Agility Quiz to see where you are right now in your own agility. You can choose to track your progress over time as you grow.

Transformational Leadership Podcast: Our podcast has experts and coaching exercises for everyone.

The 15 Accelerators of Agility Tool-Kit: Download the Wired For Disruption Tool-Kit found on our website at: www.transformleaders/WiredForDisruption

Customized Book: We can create a customized book to include a Foreword and content from your organization. E-mail: Henna@TransformLeaders.tv

References

1 "World's 25 Greatest Leaders: Heroes of the Pandemic". *Fortune*. Retrieved from https://fortune.com/worlds-greatest-leaders/2020/li-wenliang/

2 "Provide unemployed workers with access to online learning". Coursera for Government. Retrieved from https://www.coursera.org/government/workforce-recovery

3 Flanders Institute for Biotechnology (February 5, 2020) Novelty speeds up learning thanks to dopamine activation. *Science Daily*, retrieved from https://www.sciencedaily.com/releases/2020/02/200205132255.htm

4 Rodriguez, Jesus (August 23, 2019) Towards Data Science, Learning to Learn: A Gentle Introduction to Meta Learning. Retrieved from https://towardsdatascience.com/learning-to-learn-a-gentle-introduction-to-meta-learning-4befb76da91a

5 Zimmer, Ben (January 17, 2019) Kondo-ing: A Guru of Organizing Becomes a Verb. *Wall Street Journal*. Retrieved from https://www.wsj.com/articles/kondo-ing-a-guru-of-organizing-becomes-a-verb-11547745648

6   Sutcliff, Mike, Narsalay, Raghav (October 18, 2019) The Two Big Reasons That Digital Transformations Fail. *Harvard Business Review*, Retrieved from https://hbr.org/2019/10/the-two-big-reasons-that-digital-transformations-fail

7   Lerner, Jennifer S., Li, Ye, Valdesolo, Piercarlo, and Kassam, Karim S. (January 2015). Emotion and Decision-Making. *Annual Review of Psychology*. Retrieved from https://www.annualreviews.org/doi/full/10.1146/annurev-psych-010213-115043#_i6

8   Wild, Barbara, Erb, Michael, Barteis, Mathias (June 1, 2001) Are emotions contagious? Evoked emotions while viewing emotionally expressive faces: quality, quantity, time course and gender differences. *Psychiatry Research*, Volume 102, Issue 2, pp 109-124. Retrieved from https://www.sciencedirect.com/science/article/abs/pii/S0165178101002256

9   Connelly, Mark (August 30, 2018) Kubler-Ross Five Stage Model. *Change Management Coach*. Retrieved from https://www.change-management-coach.com/kubler-ross.html

10 Sampson, Stacey (June 28, 2017) Everything You Need to Know About the Vagus Nerve. *Medical News Today*. Retrieved from https://www.medicalnewstoday.com/articles/318128

11 Ibid.

References

12 Brains Can Be Trained in Compassion, Study Shows, (May 22, 2013) *Association for Psychological Science*. Retrieved from https://www.psychologicalscience.org/news/releases/compassion-training.html

13 Taren, Adrienne A., Creswell, David J., Gianaros, Peter J., (May 22, 2013). Dispositional Mindfulness Co-Varies with Smaller Amygdala and Caudate Volumes in Community Adults. *PLoS ONE 8(5): e64574*. Retrieved from https://doi.org/10.1371/journal.pone.0064574.

14 Boyatzis, Richard E., Rochford, Kylie, Jack, Anthony I., (March 4, 2014) Antagonistic neural networks underlying differentiated leadership roles. *Frontiers in Human Neuroscience*, Retrieved from https://www.frontiersin.org/articles/10.3389/fnhum.2014.00114/full

15 Zak, Paul J., (June 6, 2018) How Oxytocin Can Make Your Job More Meaningful. *Workplace*. Retrieved from https://greatergood.berkeley.edu/article/item/how_oxytocin_can_make_your_job_more_meaningful

16 Scharmer, Otto, u.lab: Leading From the Emerging Future. Retrieved from https://courses.edx.org/courses/course-v1:MITx+15.671.1x+3T2019/course/

17 Snowden, David J., Boone, Mary E. (September 2007). A Leader's Framework for Decision Making. *Harvard Business Review*. Retrieved from https://hbr.org/2007/11/a-leaders-framework-for-decision-making

18 Bryce, Emma (November 9, 2019) *Live Science*. How Many Calories Can the Brain Burn by Thinking? Retrieved from https://www.livescience.com/burn-calories-brain.html

19 Ibid.

20 Wimmer, R., Schmitt, L., Davidson, T. *et al.* (2015). Thalamic Control of Sensory Selection in Divided Attention. *Nature*. Issue 526, pp 705–709. Retrieved from https://doi.org/10.1038/nature15398

21 Harvard Medical School. (August, 2018). Protect Your Brain from Stress. *Harvard Health Publishing*, Retrieved from https://www.health.harvard.edu/mind-and-mood/protect-your-brain-from-stress

22 List of Cognitive Biases, Wikipedia, retrieved from https://en.wikipedia.org/wiki/List_of_cognitive_biases

23 Berger, Jennifer Garvey (January 29, 2019) Unlocking Leadership Mindtraps: How to Thrive in Complexity. San Francisco: Stanford University Press, p2, Retrieved from https://www.amazon.com/Unlocking-Leadership-Mindtraps-Thrive-Complexity/dp/1503609014

References 131

24 Framingham, Jane (October 13, 2018) Rorschach Inkblot Test, PsychCentral. Retrieved from https://psychcentral.com/lib/rorschach-inkblot-test/

25 James, Geoffrey, How Steve Jobs Trained His Own Brain, Inc., Retrieved from https://www.inc.com/geoffrey-james/how-steve-jobs-trained-his-own-brain.html

26 Gotink, Rinske A., Meijboom, Rozanna, Vernooij, Meike W., Smits, Marion, Hunink, Myriam M.G., (October 2016), 8-week Mindfulness Based Stress Reduction Induces Brain Changes Similar to Traditional Long-Term Meditation Practice - A Systematic Review. *National Library of Medicine*. Retrieved from https://pubmed.ncbi.nlm.nih.gov/27429096/

27 Jesuthasan, Ravin, Malcolm, Tracey, Cantrell, Susan (April 22, 2020) How the Coronavirus Crisis Is Redefining Jobs. *Harvard Business Review*. Retrieved from https://hbr-org.cdn.ampproject.org/c/s/hbr.org/amp/2020/04/how-the-coronavirus-crisis-is-redefining-jobs

28 How Top Food Companies Are Responding to Changing Consumer Habits. (March 23, 2020). Retrieved from https://finance.yahoo.com/news/food-distribution-sector-responding-change-231027291.html

29 Hastwell, Claire (September 12, 2019) The Business Returns on High-Trust Work Culture, Great Place to Work. Retrieved from https://www.greatplacetowork.com/resources/blog/the-business-returns-on-high-trust-work-culture

30 Zak, Paul J., (June 6, 2018) How Oxytocin Can Make Your Job More Meaningful. *Greater Good Magazine*, Retrieved from https://greatergood.berkeley.edu/article/item/how_oxytocin_can_make_your_job_more_meaningful

31 Terris, Elizabeth T., Beavin, Laura E., Barraza, Jorge A., Schloss, Jeff, Zak, Paul J., (March 5, 2018) Endogenous Oxytocin Release Eliminates In-Group Bias in Monetary Transfers with Perspective-Taking. *Frontiers in Behavioral Neuroscience*, Retrieved from https://www.frontiersin.org/articles/10.3389/fnbeh.2018.00035/full

32 The Arbinger Institute (July 2015) The Anatomy of Peace: Resolving the Heart of Conflict. San Francisco: Berrett-Koehler Publishers. Retrieved from https://www.amazon.com/Anatomy-Peace-Resolving-Heart-Conflict/dp/1626564310

33 Covey, Stephen M.R. (February 2008) The Speed of Trust. FrankCovey Publishing. Retrieved from https://www.amazon.com/SPEED-TRUST-Thing-Changes-Everything/dp/1416549005

34 Loneliness and the Work Place: 2020 U.S. Report,

Cigna Behavioral Health, Inc. Retrieved from https://www.cigna.com/static/www-cigna-com/docs/about-us/newsroom/studies-and-reports/combatting-loneliness/cigna-2020-loneliness-report.pdf

35 Freeman, Jonathan B., Stolier, Ryan M., Ingbretsen, Zachary A., Hehman, Eric A., (August 6, 2014) Amygdala Responsivity to High-Level Social Information from Unseen Faces. *The Journal of Neuroscience.* Retrieved from http://psych.nyu.edu/freemanlab/pubs/2014Freeman_JNeuro.pdf

36 Lencioni, Parick (April 11, 2002) The Five Dysfunctions of a Team. San Francisco: Jossey-Bass, p 56. Retrieved from https://www.amazon.com/Five-Dysfunctions-Team-Leadership-Fable/dp/0787960756/ref=redir_mobile_desktop?ie=UTF8&aaxitk=HSvovg2V7dv5IcRIDuT-9Q&hsa_cr_id=3861155770301&ref_=sb_s_sparkle

37 Delistraty, Cody C. (November 2, 2014) The Psychological Comforts of Storytelling. *The Atlantic Magazine.* Retrieved from https://www.theatlantic.com/health/archive/2014/11/the-psychological-comforts-of-storytelling/381964/

38 Fredrickson, Barbara L. (December 2013). Love 2.0: Finding Happiness and Health in Moments of Connection. New York: Penguin Publishing. Retrieved from https://www.amazon.com/Love-2-0-Finding-Happiness-Connection/dp/0142180475

39 Gallup Q&A with Tom Rath and Barry Conchie (January 8, 2009) What Followers Want from Leaders. Retrieved from https://news.gallup.com/businessjournal/113542/what-followers-want-from-leaders.aspx

40 Nadella, Satya (March 21, 2020) Coming Together to Combat COVID-19. Retrieved from https://www.linkedin.com/pulse/coming-together-combat-covid-19-satya-nadella/

41 Video: A Message to Marriott International Associates from President and CEO Arne Sorenson (March 20, 2020). Retrieved from https://www.hospitalitynet.org/news/4097646.html

42 Business Roundtable (August 19, 2019) Business Roundtable Redefines the Purpose of a Corporation to Promote 'An Economy That Serves All Americans'. Retrieved from https://www.businessroundtable.org/business-roundtable-redefines-the-purpose-of-a-corporation-to-promote-an-economy-that-serves-all-americans

43 Ibid.

44 Kim, Suntae, Matthew, Karlesky J., Myers, Christopher G., Schifelling, Todd (June 16, 2016). Companies Are Becoming B-Corporations. *Harvard Business Review*. Retrieved from https://hbr.org/2016/06/why-companies-are-becoming-b-

References

corporations

45 Fortune. World's 25 Greatest Leaders: Heroes of the Pandemic (2020). Retrieved from https://fortune.com/worlds-greatest-leaders/2020/

46 Andy Fink, BlackRock CEO letter: A Fundamental Reshaping of Finance. Retrieved from https://www.blackrock.com/corporate/investor-relations/larry-fink-ceo-letter

47 Scharmer, Otto, Kaufer, Katrin (April 29, 2013) Leading From The Emerging Future. San Francisco: Berrett-Koehler. Retrieved from www.presencing.org/assets/images/theory-u/Ego_to_Eco_Intro.pdf

48 World Economic Forum (January 22, 2020) The Reskilling Revolution: Better Skills, Better Jobs, Better Education for a Billion People by 2030. Retrieved from https://www.weforum.org/press/2020/01/the-reskilling-revolution-better-skills-better-jobs-better-education-for-a-billion-people-by-2030

49 University of Wisconsin. The Triple Bottom Line. Retrieved from https://sustain.wisconsin.edu/sustainability/triple-bottom-line/

50 Shah, Dharmesh. The HubSpot Culture Code: Creating a Company We Love. *HubSpot*. Retrieved

from https://blog.hubspot.com/blog/tabid/6307/bid/34234/The-HubSpot-Culture-Code-Creating-a-Company-We-Love.aspx

Printed in Great Britain
by Amazon